Leaders Praise *Finding the UP in the Downturn*

"In these challenging economic times, all of us need to stay focused and motivated in order to succeed. Fawn's book gives us the nourishment we need – she hits us squarely in the eyes with practical advice and useful reminders. She urges us to leave behind any "woe is me" thinking, get up, dust ourselves off and put ourselves in a position to win. I encourage you to keep this book handy and read it for a regular reminder on the importance of an "I Can" mentality. Take charge of your destiny, be confident, dream often and big."
Mike Salzberg, *President, Campbell Sales Company, a $3.2 billion wing of the Campbell Soup Company*

"For many, the current downturn in our economy is a new experience. Without the proper mindset and perspective it is easy to lose hope. *Finding the UP in the Downturn* gives us power to persevere during the darkest times and guides us into the light of better times. This is absolutely a *must* read."
Elizabeth Baker, *Senior Vice President of Strategic Initiatives, SAP*

"WOW. Fawn is terrific, she absolutely understands the issues. More important, she knows how to truly connect with men and women to help them understand how to capture opportunities and challenge themselves. Fawn's realism comes across both as a speaker and author. She has lived her lessons and her honesty makes a difference."
Kathy Hannan, *Managing Partner, KPMG*

"Fawn Germer's powerful points about taking initiative and overcoming obstacles are outstanding. Her down-to-earth style, personal experiences and sense of humor drive her message home."
Paulo Costa, *fmr. CEO, Novartis*

"Fawn has had a tremendous impact on my life. She gets right to what really matters. She touches an emotional chord that pushes us out of our comfort zones. Her real life stories help all of us to realize that our shortcomings can turn out to be our greatest gifts. She challenges us to take risks and pull ourselves to a level we never thought we dared to go."
Marie Quintana, *VP, Multicultural Sales, PepsiCo*

"Having seen Fawn Germer speak, I expected a lot. *Finding the UP in the Downturn* delivers the hope and direction we need to get moving in spite of tough times. She inspires others to take risks...To push their limits. To step out of their comfort zone… To achieve more than they might have thought possible... To be the best they can be."
Maureen McGurl, *fmr. Executive Vice President. The Stop & Shop Supermarket Company.*

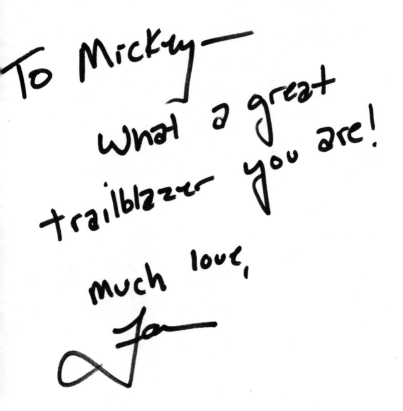

To Micky—
What a great
trailblazer you are!

much love,

FINDING THE UP IN THE DOWNTURN

HOW TO TURN THE ECONOMIC MELTDOWN INTO YOUR GREATEST OPPORTUNITY

By Fawn Germer

Newhouse Books

©Copyright 2009 by Newhouse Books and Fawn Germer. All rights reserved.
First edition April, 2009

Finding the UP in the Downturn
How to Turn The Economic Meltdown Into Your Greatest Opportunity
Germer, Fawn.
Library of Congress Control Number: 2009901235

Other titles by Fawn Germer:
Hard Won Wisdom, Perigee Books, 2001
Mustang Sallies, Perigee Books, 2004
Mermaid Mambo, Newhouse Books, 2007
The NEW Woman Rules, Network Books, 2007

www.fawngermer.com or her blog at www.hardwonwisdom.com.
Speaking information: info@fawngermer.com or (727) 467-0202.

Newhouse Books
Printed in the United States of America

ISBN 978-0-9795466-9-3

All rights reserved. No part of this book may be reproduced in any form or
by any electronic or mechanical means including information storage and
retrieval systems without permission in writing from the publisher or author,
except by a reviewer, who may quote brief passages in a review.

Edited by Barbara Jiannetti

Cover design by Barbara Willard

"For my Uncle Chuck,
  who has always been there for me."

Contents

Acknowledgments

Thanks to my mother, Betty Germer – who has inspired me every day of my life. To my father, Fred Germer, the good optimist, who blessed me with hope and confidence.

Thanks to Julie Hipp, who encouraged me to hurry up and do this. And the brain trust: Nancy Krawczyk, Kim Feil, Sandra Bushby, Helayne Angelus, Joan Toth, Luci Sheehan, Bobbie O'Hare, Bob Silverstein, Rebecca Whitley, Suzann Clark, Mike Gorshe, Lloyd Sineni and my friends at the Network of Executive Women.

Thanks to my incredible editor, Barb Jiannetti, photographer Lisa Presnail, stylist Dana Alford, title master Connie Bouchard, marketing whiz Art Fyvolent and cover designer Barb Willard.

Thanks to my dear friend, the late Kerri Susan Smith, who pushed me to persevere when I encountered so many obstacles getting my first book published, and was the one who suggested I become a professional speaker. I owe her so much and will miss her forever.

Thanks to my friends who share this great ride with me. I am so lucky.

And thanks to my readers, who teach me more than I could ever teach them.

Introduction

"Why do they keep calling it a 'recession'?" my friend asked. "It's a DEPRESSION."

I have to agree the word is fitting. Regardless of how the economists classify it, Americans are depressed. They have lost hope for the future. There is a constant vibe of fear and worry.

If it is starting to get to you, breathe deeply. As the economy collapses, we actually have our greatest opportunity to innovate and be successful. When others give up, they move to the sidelines and clear the way for the daring among us to charge ahead. Whether you want to gain ground in your corporate job, have recently been laid off, or are flirting with starting a business, there *is* opportunity out there. But success in this environment requires a change in perspective. It requires a fortitude you likely have never had to muster.

More than anything, it requires you to take control over the negative messages that are filling your brain.

If you are in the workplace, you can expand your power and position by demonstrating leadership and being part of the solution -- not the problem. Now is the time to stand up and lead.

Instead of looking at the number of failing businesses and deciding to hold off on starting your own, you can use the bad economy to negotiate killer rents, deals on equipment, cheaper labor, etc.

Finally, if you've lost your job, don't give up without a fight. Pick yourself up and put yourself out front as you compete for the positions that are out there.

The Bottom Line

1. When you expect the worst, you get it.

2. When everyone else gives up, the window is wide open for those who don't.

3. If you give yourself an inch to fail, you will fail.

4. There is an upside to every downturn. We can create profit from the failing economy.

5. You never know how close you are to turning the corner until you turn the corner. Move forward an inch at a time if you have to, just do *not* quit.

6. The greatest leaders in history all emerged from adversity. This is a great moment to prove your mettle.

7. Hyper-perform to create visibility and viability in the workplace.

8. When you fall down, get back up!

All is not lost. In fact, if you do this right, you have everything to gain.

Change Your Mindset

Stocks Slump As Signs Point To Harder Times

By Neil Irwin and David Cho
Washington Post Staff Writers

"Businesses cut prices at a record rate and builders started fewer new homes last month than anytime on record, according to new government data, as the outlook for the economy continues to dim.

"The data helped spur another terrible day for the stock market, as did a projection of more hard times ahead by leaders of the Federal Reserve.

"The stock market fell another 5 percent, as measured by the Dow Jones industrial average, which closed below 8,000 for the first time in this bear market. New-home starts in were the lowest since at least 1959, when the government began keeping data. The consumer price index plummeted by the most since that series of monthly data was started in 1947, as the economy slowed so abruptly that companies had to slash prices to sell products.

"And Federal Reserve leaders released projections indicating they expect the economy to worsen significantly in the coming year. The most pessimistic of 17 Fed officials expects joblessness to rise to 8 percent at the end of 2009, which would be the highest in a quarter-century..."

When you read that kind of news, there's one natural human reaction.

You freeze up.

You become scared.

You worry that what you have right now is all that you will ever have.

You worry if you spend twenty dollars at a restaurant instead of staying home and cooking macaroni and cheese, you'll have nothing later on.

Forgive my absolute optimism here. I know that times have never been tougher for our generation. I get it. In today's mail, I received a $350 electric bill, a $560 health insurance invoice and a $130 water bill. What will be in tomorrow's mail? More of the same.

I get it. I get it!

I could go on and on and on about it, but I don't because everyone else is going down that dark road, worrying about what's wrong, obsessing about what might happen, fearing what is next, questioning how they'll even survive. While they do that, I travel down another path.

I just say one thing: "I'd better make sure I make good money this year."

Keep it positive.

What happens when one day of bad news is replaced by another day of even worse news? We become psychologically beleaguered and start to expect the worse. When we expect the worst, surprise! We get it.

Why go there? Why travel the dark road when you don't have to?

If you think you won't get much business this year, guess what? You won't get much business this year. If you believe you are going to have real money problems, you're going to have real money problems. If you think you won't be able to find a job, just keep lining up for that unemployment check.

But, remember this: When everyone else is giving up, there is a huge window of opportunity for those of us who aren't.

This is a great moment to break from the pack, run fast and win big.

Think about it. When everyone else wallows in negativity, their collective performance suffers. What a moment to stand out. For those of us who choose not to buy into the defeatism, there is an opening to create real success. This downturn has a real upside for those who choose to actively and aggressively advance themselves.

Companies are crying out for good leadership from the middle ranks and the top. Industry is desperate for innovation. This bad economy has created wild bargains for those who are ready to invest in others or create their own new businesses. For almost every negative, there is a positive.

Lead. Innovate. Invest. Believe.

If you are set on using this moment to create greater success for yourself, you have got to tune out the negative messages that are assailing your confidence on a daily basis. It is too easy to be consumed by negativity when you get a daily dose of doom on the front page, on your television set, over the radio and via the Internet. It is a constant downer message telling you how bad you've got it and how much worse it is going to get. If you buy into it, you might as well just give up and get in a bread line.

If you check the news faithfully, you can't feel uplifted. It's just too heavy. People openly fret that they will lose their savings, that their retirement funds will be looted, that there won't be a dime left to fund their Social Security and that they will have to work until the day they die. Their minds go into negativity loops and they become consumed with worry. The more they worry, the more real their fears become.

And yet...

Look around you. Even in this terrible economy, people are still consumers of goods and services. They *have* to spend money. There is business out there! There is opportunity. Most people have cut back, but they are still consuming. Life has not ended. As things continue to chug along, you can either focus on the decline or head into the zone of possibility that still exists – and really make a mark.

I am not so upbeat that I close my eyes to the reality of the terrible adversity that has overwhelmed so many people. But I have decided not to be one of the victims of this economy, and you can make that same decision. You can make money, advance your career and have a successful journey in a time like this. You can operate in a zone of growth and abundance, regardless of what is happening to everyone else.

You can do that, or you can buy into all the negativity and struggle all you want. It's your choice.

Whether your business is selling real estate or cruise vacations or cell phone service or carpeting or anything else, *somebody* is closing deals. *Somebody* is doing something.

Make up your mind that, if *somebody* is going to succeed, it is going to be *you.*

Take Charge of Your Brain

I cannot stand the B.S. that comes straight from the mouths of motivational speakers and author gurus who seem better suited for the sale of used cars than helping others. So when I bring up the subject of the "Law of Attraction," realize that this principle had to go through quite a test to get by me. I am a natural-born doubter.

Several years ago, as I was starting my business, I was told to get Napoleon Hill's classic 1937 book, *Think and Grow Rich.* The title made me cringe. As a recovering journalist, I felt like I should hide the book in a brown paper bag. Cynics and skeptics *never* buy books with titles like that, but I was doing exactly that.

It took a long time for me to digest the power of Hill's message, but once I did, it helped me to create more wealth and success than I'd ever imagined. With Andrew Carnegie as his mentor, Hill gained access to all the great entrepreneurs of his time and got their formulas for achievement. They taught him to manifest success and wealth by writing his own future. From those interviews, he came up with thirteen core principles that help individuals to achieve at the highest possible level. The bottom line: You create your reality, and you do it through the messages you program into your brain with your self-talk. If you imagine you will wind up sick, old, broke and alone, you'll retire sick, old, broke and alone. But, if you tell yourself that you will retire with great wealth, then follow-through with hard work fueled by unrelenting persistence, faith and a burning desire to succeed, you'll retire with great wealth. You can write your future if you can turn off your cynicism and just go with it.

It took awhile for me to fully understand and appreciate that. But, every time I allow myself to expect difficulty, I get difficulty.

The first time I had a great year as a speaker, I eyed my success with skepticism. I was suddenly making more in a month than I used to make in a year, and I said to myself, "Wow. There's no way I'll be able to do this again next year.

Guess what?

I didn't.

And when I started complaining about how miserable I was traveling because of my busy speaking business, guess what happened?

My travel dried up.

No travel, no business. No business, no money.

Now I just say, "I am going to make great money this year!" And, "I love travel because it means business is good!"

So far, so good.

Think and grow rich. I get it.

Much has been made about the recent book and DVD for *The Secret,* which is all about the Law of Attraction. At first, I had a problem with *The Secret* because I thought it was stolen straight out of Hill's work, but I looked into it and found that Hill wasn't the first to write about it. There were others. Many others. The concept of the Law of Attraction is even in the Bible.

So now I don't care who came up with the concept. I don't care where you learn about it. What matters is that you open yourself to the power you have, then create your own powerful reality. It is so simple that it seems improbable. But, you will think tens of thousands of thoughts every day. Why not use those thoughts to direct you toward your greatest success? Feel certain you will win. Know what you are creating for yourself, and then follow through with actions that manifest your vision.

I've interviewed more than 200 great leaders and trailblazers for my other books. So many of them have told me that we are all capable of doing anything we want to do – if we *really* want to do it. That's what this is all about.

These are tough times, but they present us with great chances to excel and achieve. If you don't buy into that truth – then follow through with the right self-talk – you will be just like the multitudes of Americans who see scarcity and obstacles rather than abundance and opportunity.

What Have You Been Telling Yourself?

Ski instructors will tell that if you look at a dangerous black-diamond run below you and try to figure out how the heck you will be able to maneuver it, you'll fall down.

Just ski.

Do it, don't over think or overanalyze it. Let go and ski.

Just go.

We don't do that with our lives, do we? We see what looks like a treacherous path ahead of us and talk ourselves out of trying to cross it before we even start. We are so afraid to trust our abilities that we choose instead to limit ourselves.

Some people classify themselves as "average" or "middle class" or "worker bees" or "mid-level managers." If you label yourself, you limit yourself. You choose to set yourself apart from those who succeed at the highest levels. It's almost like you are mentally delineating the career "haves" and the career "have nots," literally choosing to place yourself with the "have nots" because you don't see yourself with the same potential and possibility that the superstars exhibit.

The same thing goes for all of us as we grapple with the looming negative economic forces at play. How many people are operating in a zone of fear, worrying they might be victims, wondering how they will even survive? MOST PEOPLE! Does that kind of negativity position them for great success? Of course not.

It is amazing how people choose to shut themselves out of opportunity by being pessimistic and lacking confidence.

There will always be someone smarter than you are. And someone who isn't as smart. There will always be someone with more savvy – and less. Someone with better intellectual instincts – and worse. Someone who is more creative – and less. Do you have to wait until you are the best in every category before you can see yourself as capable of achieving at the highest level? No. You will never win all the marbles. You don't have to. You just need to focus your vision, make up your mind and go out and do the work. Remind yourself again and again that the people who succeed are not the best or the brightest. They are the boldest.

Just be bold!

Especially now, because boldness will carry you a long way in this climate of fear. Everyone else is too afraid to see what's out there. This adversity is a big break for those who have the psychological fortitude to hang in there, strategize and go for it.

Turn Off the News

If you put bad news in its place, the world is not quite so dark.

What I am about to suggest is heresy, considering my past as a journalist who harshly judged those who chose to be ignorant of current events. But, considering the circumstances today, ignorance is bliss. Minimize your exposure.

When you hear bad news, you expect bad news. When you are told again and again that all is lost, all is lost. Enough, already! Start tuning the negativity out. Have a general idea of what is going on, but make a conscious decision to mute the volume and frequency of the pessimism because, otherwise, the dire predictions of the media analysts will swallow you up.

Affirmations to Get You In the Game

1. Every obstacle presents a new opportunity for me to succeed.

2. The window is wide open for me to step in and achieve while others give up.

3. This is a great chance to show leadership and expand my influence.

4. I am creating a richer and more abundant life.

5. I am going to make more money than I have ever made.

6. I choose to focus on the possibility that exists and I know that life will continue to be abundant.

7. I have faith in myself and know I will emerge from this experience more successful than I ever dreamed I'd be.

8. I am more confident every day.

Even if these are the worst of times for millions of people, they are not the worst of times for *all* people. Those of us who are adept at finding opportunity in moments of great adversity will create success for ourselves, regardless of what the market does. Maybe we will have to change what we do or how we do it, but successful people have the confidence to know that they will figure it out.

There is a lot of talk about the tough times we are going through. Too much talk. Even if it is real, the negativity is powerful. Don't buy into the notion that you are experiencing a moment of great scarcity, rather than wild abundance. Your ability to manifest abundance for yourself depends entirely on your ability to convince your brain that abundance is attainable.

Science has proven that all of us have great power to do that, if we just get with the program. The brain is like a computer. It works according to program. If you program it with fear, doubt and negativity, it will function in a realm of fear, doubt and negativity. But, if you program it to respond with strength, confidence and positivism, guess what? Your brain will direct you to operate in a realm of strength, confidence and positivism. Your brain believes whatever you tell it to believe.

Put the bad news in check. Know that things are tough, but

don't obsess about it. At the same time, don't delude yourself. This is not the time to buy yourself a Hummer if you don't have stacks of cash in the bank. But, this *is* the time for you to live a rich, full life. Just protect yourself from getting sucked under by the negativity. You are learning to use these tough moments to create *more* success, rather than fighting so hard to just maintain and sustain yourself.

The window is open. Opportunity is here. If you see only adversity, you will experience adversity. Take control over the negativity by tuning out the pessimism and going about the business of creating more success for yourself.

Leaving Average Behind

I can still hear my mother's voice.

"You can do better than this."

I was in the tenth grade and I had brought home a report card with a few As, a couple of Bs, a C and a D – the only D I'd ever gotten – in geometry. I didn't see anything wrong with that report card because it wasn't much different from what my friends were bringing home.

But, Mom did see something wrong with it.

"You are not average," she said, "so you can't bring home a report card like this. If you were average, it would be all right. If I knew this was the best you could do, it would be all right. But, it isn't the best you can do and you know it."

I hadn't really thought about it before, whether I was smart or talented or anything else. I was just a kid who wanted desperately to fit in despite being hindered by a major case of nerdiness. I *wanted* to be average because then I would blend in with the others. Hanging there with mediocrity seemed like a pretty safe way to get through high school.

If you think about it, I was right. People find comfort in the middle at the workplace because mediocrity appears to be a very safe place to hang. You don't have to deal with the risk of being extreme – either too excellent or too poor. You aren't a problem child that needs to be put on probation or dealt with. You aren't a model of excellence who is a target for people who are jealous or threatened. You're just in the crowd.

That doesn't work now. We'll look at this in much greater depth later on, but this is a time when companies don't need average performers – and are getting rid of them by the thousands. It is a time for you to dig deep and deliver. If you haven't done that in the past, it is time to make the mental decision to do it now. Regardless of your track record, it is time to reposition yourself as a go-to person who delivers every time. And, you can do that.

I had to do that with geometry.

My mother's tone of voice made it very clear that I would be making a few changes with regard to my academic approach.

It's amazing how quickly I turned things around after that lecture. All A's, and even a B in geometry. I just had to make the decision.

I've had to make that decision again and again throughout my career. It *is* a conscious decision to ratchet things up another notch, to produce more, to concentrate harder, to work longer – to deliver. It *is* a decision to leave the pack and be excellent.

But, if you want to thrive – especially during this downturn -- you've got to ask yourself what you want for yourself.

Are you going to be one of the victims of this mess? Or are you going to make up your mind to be one of the victors? Are you going to surrender or fight?

You have more options than you know. Just make the decision to get your head in the game.

The Window Is Wide Open. It Is Your Moment.

There are three options when things begin to sour: 1) Give up 2) Follow the leader 3) Take the lead. One thing you can bet is that these tough times will end. They always do. So, who will wind up winning when it's all over? The individuals who showed courage and vision and were relentless in trying to make a difference. The ones who decided that, no matter how many times they fell down, they would get up again, ready to fight.

If you breathe in the despair that is in the air, you will breathe out that negativity in your performance. Don't let it happen. You will be fine. You are smart and capable. WAKE UP! – GET IN THE GAME! A downturn is an upturn if you get your mindset in check.

If you are banking on the government or some politician or the passage of time to make things right for you, you are making a huge mistake. YOU are the only variable that you can control. You can't control what other people do or how the market will react. But, you *can* control what *you* do and how *you* react. How are you going to get in front of this situation and be a trusted, go-to contributor? What do you have to offer? How can you make things easier for your colleagues and bosses? What can you do for your customers that no one else is doing?

Your self-confidence and your abilities will inspire others to have confidence in you. That will bolster your leadership finesse and get others to invest in you. If you win their trust and faith, you will be able to accomplish so much more than if you act alone.

So, before we begin this process, I want to explore the steps you will take in order to gain ground when everyone else is falling behind.

> **Look around.** Be visionary enough to see where you can make the difference that will either propel you financially or give you more experience or clout to help you later on.

> **Shut down the negativity.** If you see bad times, you will experience bad times. You don't have to live in a world of denial or make-believe, but shove the negativity off to the side and train yourself to always

see the opportunities that arise out of adversity. Be first on the scene to grab the gold, *because there is gold out there.*

Work harder than you have ever worked. Whatever you were doing before won't be enough if you want to profit from these challenging times. If you were already overworked, you may roll your eyes at the notion that you must do more, but you must do more. All of us have been through times when we have had to exert Herculean effort in order to either make a deadline or master some challenge. This is a time for that kind of sustained effort.

Stand out. By working harder, delivering excellence and taking the lead, you are a valuable player – either to your current boss or to some other company that is looking for good talent. Those who blend in risk being dumped on when there is more work to be assigned or cut out when layoffs come.

Be seen as part of the solution – not the problem. This makes you valuable to others who can't lead alone.

Over deliver. You don't want to be tagged as "below average," because you will be punished for it and possibly expended. You don't want to be seen as "average," because you'll be dumped on and pushed around. "Above average" is good, because the powers that be will, at least, think twice before messing with you. But, don't stop there. If you are seen as consistently excellent and productive, you will emerge as a go-to person who will help create a stronger future for your company. These are uncertain times where cuts are unpredictable, but you can take steps to protect yourself by exhibiting hard work, extreme confidence, great attitude and a desire to contribute.

Take nothing for granted. You are not indispensable– no matter how smart you are, no matter how much you contribute, no matter how long you've been there. These are weird times. But, there is great power in knowing, deep down, that you will be fine – regardless of what transpires in one place of business. Keep networking so you know what other opportunities exist and the people who can plug you into them.

Get your head in the game. If your mind is filled with doubt, fear and negativity, CHANGE YOUR MIND.

Go There

The unrelenting barrage of negativity wears on all of us.

Right about the time of the cascading reports of company layoffs, I looked at my calendar for the coming year and thought, "At least I have booked enough work to get me through '09. I can make it on that much money." Like there would not be another check in the mail, regardless of what I did with my time.

WAIT A MINUTE.

Why on *earth* would I let a thought like that enter my head? Why would anyone? Do you know what that kind of thinking creates?

It creates limits.

Every time I expect a negative outcome – I get one. Every time I let negativity or self-doubt challenge any element of my success, I stop succeeding. I have learned to take responsibility for my thinking and take power over my thoughts. What am I doing to put that negative thought in its place? Kick myself in the rear-end and start moving. I'm expanding my marketing plan. And I am moving forward with certainty that this will be, by far, my best year yet. It will be.

There will be ups and downs and all kinds of challenges, but I am so ready for them. Are you?

Success is so incredibly mental. When you see so many other people feeling hopeless, you start to feel hopeless yourself. But you can take steps to ward it off proactively.

When you fear that good times will not last or that adversity will hinder your endeavors, you begin to operate out of a "lack" modality, not a realm of "abundance." I know a lot of people think it is Pollyanna talk to be preaching abundance when there is so much talk of our collapsing economy, but I know something for a fact: The minute I start operating out of lack, all of the abundance I have disappears. And when that happens, it is all my fault. My attitude is one thing I can control.

Just because you adhere to the principles of abundance through the Law of Attraction (that our thoughts create our reality), it does not mean you will be spared your share of obstacles and adversity. But, if you are certain you will prevail, you will prevail. It is that simple and that true.

If you get knocked down but are certain you will bounce right back up, you will bounce right back up. But, if you get knocked down and expect to stay down for awhile, you'll stay down.

After that negative thought about getting no more business entered my mind this morning, I had to take a moment to correct my course. One negative thought is no big deal, but a negative thought that imagines my whole next year as a washout needs to be addressed. I have no room for that kind of thinking in my life because I want the next year to be my most successful ever.

How will I do that? With this book. With shrewd marketing.

With a great game plan. With the help of my network. With the support of my friends.

How will you?

Every time the masses surrender to negativity and give up, it creates tremendous opportunity for those of us who don't. My job is to look at my industry and see where the window is open. How can I create more success with the skills and knowledge I have? How can I gain ground in the speaking industry when budget cuts will drastically reduce the number of conferences and events? By turning out this book on a timetable that makes me one of the first speakers to deal with this issue for this economy. Instead of hunkering down and finding a way to get by with diminishing revenues, I'm going to figure out how to *grow* my business and *expand* my revenues by serving the needs created by this crisis. My challenge is to make sure I adapt my game plan to take advantage of the opportunities that still exist.

I'm in charge here. I can create good times or bad. There obviously are things I can't control. But there are also things I *can* control. The most important thing I can control is what I allow my head to think. The same goes for you.

Here is how you can strategize yourself to succeed in the bleakest of times. Pay close attention to your thoughts about your immediate future. Do you expect abundance or struggle? If you expect struggle, what do you think you are going to get? Struggle. So, start telling yourself, "I will create abundance." If you hear yourself saying, "Everyone else is struggling," remind yourself, "I am not like everyone else." Expect good things. Feel certain that you have what it takes to steer your way through any difficulties. Know that tough times are temporary and that you are smart enough to persevere through *anything.*

How to Make Your Thoughts Work for You

Monitor your thoughts. Be aware of what you are telling

yourself. If you catch a negative thought, quickly rewrite it and repeat the positive version numerous times to drown out the naysaying voice.

Write and repeat affirmations. The fastest way to end the negativity is to overpower it with better thoughts. Affirmations are a tremendous tool. Write down five positive affirmations to carry you through your challenges and repeat them often. Your first day, say them at least 100 times. The second day, 50 times. The third day, 25 times. After that, say them at least three to 10 times a day until you are saying them naturally and automatically. Some simple examples are:

1. I am creating my greatest success.

2. I am quickly adapting and taking actions that will make me even more successful.

3. These are good times.

4. I think only positive thoughts and live a positive life.

5. I will be fine.

6. I am smart enough to win under any circumstances.

7. This is a great opportunity for me to create even more success.

8. I look ahead with confidence.

Consider the company you are keeping. You certainly have to be there for your friends as they face their own difficulties, but if their negativity is weighing you down, take action. Either minimize the amount of time you are exposed to the negativity or set some boundaries with your friends, telling them that it is too easy to get caught up in pessimism and you want to keep things positive.

End the Doomsday thinking. There is no "all or nothing" in any of this. Don't allow yourself to contemplate the worst-case scenario because it is highly unlikely it will happen. You've been around long enough to see your friends and acquaintances encounter tough times, but you haven't seen them eating out of garbage pails and sleeping on the streets. It's not going to happen to you. Don't entertain those possibilities.

Ride the roller coaster. There's an old cliché that "Tough times don't last. Tough people do." If you are tough, you can find ways to succeed and thrive regardless of the obstacles of the day. Wouldn't you rather develop the tools that will help you through this tough round – and the next – instead of giving up or giving in? These difficulties are just the latest challenges in a lifetime of challenge. Don't be a wimp about it.

Laugh at yourself. When you hear yourself saying or thinking things that are not positive or constructive, shut yourself up! Tell yourself, "Stop being a worry wart!" Or, "There you go again. Get crackin'! You're going to be so successful!"

Excuses Don't Count. Results Do.

If you are looking for excuses of why you can't be successful or why you can't do what you want to do, you won't have to look far these days. Excuses abound.

Nobody's hiring. Everybody's firing.

You're too young. You're too old.

Blah, blah, blah.

I still hold to the belief that, if you aren't doing what you really want to be doing, it's because you really don't want to do it.

There is so much in life that you can't control, right? Maybe there *is* something else to blame. My first career was as a newspaper reporter and I am watching all of my old friends scrambling to recreate themselves as their industry dies. They can't do the work

> Excuse: You're too old to do something different.
>
> *Bull.*
> *Grandma Moses didn't start painting American folk art until her late 70s. S. I. Hayakawa didn't get elected to the U.S. Senate until he was 70. When Golda Meir was elected prime minister of Israel, she was 71. George Burns didn't win an Academy Award until he was 80. George Brunstad was 70 when he swam the English Channel. Mario Curnis climbed the 29,035-foot summit of Mount Everest when he was 66. Cardinal Angelo Roncalli became Pope John XXIII when he was 76 and called Vatican II. George Selbach scored a 110-yard hole-in-one at age 96.*

they love the most in the way they want to do it. They aren't making excuses – they are facing reality. Right?

Sure. It is a fact that it is highly unlikely they will find work doing what they have always done in the way they have always done it. But there is so much they can do if they open their minds and use the creativity they have always needed for their work. The same goes for you. You might not get to play the game you want to play it, but you do get to play.

I am my greatest obstacle, and you are yours. We are also our greatest assets.

This is a moment when you can position yourself to find greatness at a time when most Americans are wallowing in weakness. It is all up to you. You know people who blame everything and everyone else for the difficulties they face. Look at all of the unfortunate people who have lost their homes to foreclosure. I feel terrible for them. They feel terrible for themselves, even though some of what happened was the result of bad decisions or bad timing on their part.

Look at the people who could have made career changes when times were better, but hesitated because they thought they had more security counting on what they already had. Again, bad decisions and bad timing.

But, we all make mistakes. This is no time to surrender to

them and declare yourself a failure. This is a time to pick up and move on, driving yourself toward a more successful and prosperous future.

If you are in a tough situation because of bad choices, get over it. You can either fret about your difficulties for the next five years or go about the business of making new success. If you have been laid off from work and can't find a job, get in the game. Find the way to compete smarter, faster and more effectively than anyone else (I'll show you how later). If you are working for a company that is on the brink of caving in, come up with a plan, either for your company or for yourself.

Own the moment. Don't just stand there – do something.

You can rattle off any number of excuses of why things won't work, but that only puts you on a path toward defeat. Times are what they are. What are you going to do?

You can do so much, once you stop limiting yourself. You are as capable as anyone else.

The world is filled with success stories from visionaries who saw possibility and lived it. We hear these stories all the time, of people who started poor and wound up rich, people who couldn't speak a word of English but wound up running major corporations.

> **Excuse: You lack the education to do something.**
>
> *Right.*
>
> *Among those who never earned college diplomas: Bill Gates, Maya Angelou, Larry Ellison, Jane Goodall, Michael Dell, Quentin Tarantino, David Geffen, Laura Ingalls Wilder, Thomas Edison, Woody Allen, Carl Bernstein, Eleanor Roosevelt, Ray Bradbury, Estee Lauder, Richard Branson, Agatha Christie, James Cameron, Grover Cleveland, Walter Cronkite, Muriel Siebert, Harry Truman, Abraham Lincoln and George Washington. In addition, Peter Jennings and John D. Rockefeller never got their high school diplomas.*

> **Excuse: You come from the wrong side of the tracks. You were raised poor..**
>
> *So were Oprah Winfrey, Benjamin Franklin, Malcolm X, Jackie Joyner-Kersey, George Orwell, Charles Dickens, Elvis Presley, Roseanne Barr, Gloria Steinem, Shania Twain, Truman Capote and millions of other successful people.*

Sometimes those examples seem so remote, like fodder for *Reader's Digest* or *USA Today* or *Forbes,* but those things always seem to happen to *other* people --other people who seem to have some sort of success microchip that must have been implanted in their brains by aliens.

But, you know there is no secret success microchip.

If you want something – really want something – you can manifest it. You just have to see it, commit to it, and work like hell to make it real.

There truly is *nothing* standing in your way except the excuses you allow.

One of the women I interviewed from the Fortune 50 Most Powerful Women in America started in the pet department at Walmart and never went to college. I know a woman running a major grocery chain who started as a bagger in the checkout line.

One of my closest friends is a former welfare mother who drove a cab to put herself through law school while caring for her two small children as a single parent. She eventually became a well-known judge, then shifted careers to pursue her dream of writing. She recently finished writing one of the best novels I've ever read.

Another of my best friends was offended when, as a secretary, a client came in and told her she had an "idiot's job." That indignity inspired her to go to medical school and eventually become one of the nation's first female forensic pathologists. She was such a trailblazer that she soon was elected coroner in a major metropolitan area, then decided she wanted to next hit the road and travel. She used her skills and passions as she unearthed the mass graves left behind in Bosnia. Not much of an idiot.

> Excuse: You're disabled.
>
> *Tom Cruise (dyslexia), Patty Duke (bipolar), Stephen Hawking (Lou Gehrig's disease), Magic Johnson (HIV), Marlee Matlin (deaf), Itzhak Perlman (paralyzed from polio), Franklin Roosevelt (paralyzed from polio).*

Don't stop trying because CBS News or the New York Times tells you that the sky is falling.

Don't stop dreaming because most everyone else is struggling.

Don't stop.

All of us have our dreams. Some people talk themselves into them; most people talk themselves out of them. But, the dreams are there.

Since you only get one shot at living, I suggest you live large, regardless of the consistent bad news you get each day. Don't hunker down in that safe zone of settling for the known when you can find true greatness by being a little bold and having a little fun.

There are plenty of excuses for inaction, but the most common one is fear. No one wants to fail, so most people won't even try. We lack the confidence to charge into change and enjoy the ride for all of its mystery and potential. So, we keep on keeping on, as boring or unchallenging as the circumstances are.

That's okay if you are truly happy with your decisions and are living a life without regrets. But, if there is even a twinge of regret nagging at you, stop making excuses and start seeking results.

How will you ever know what you are capable of doing if you don't give yourself the freedom to fail every once in awhile? If you don't fail a little, you are not testing your limits. This is the time to go out there and push as hard as you can.

The Leap

I hate those books that seem like they were written by snake oil salesmen who have the secret antidote for magic self esteem, unbridled success and limitless wealth. What a crock.

So when I talk about how thoughts determine results, realize the message is coming from a recovered cynic who was once a hard-bitten, negative reporter.

After I left journalism and decompressed a few years, I encountered others who manifested huge success with an attitude shift that could only have been possible through self-confidence and fearlessness. They believed they could achieve greatness, so they did.

I remember asking Nobel Peace Prize-winner Jody Williams what separated the individual who is ordinary from the individual who is extraordinary. "The belief that she's ordinary," she said. There is so much power and truth in that concept. You are what you think. Williams began her career as a dental assistant but won the Nobel for leading the crusade against land mines.

The biggest step in this process is the buy-in – that decision to stop rolling your eyes and start leaving disbelief and skepticism behind.

Cynicism is deadly to visionaries. It snuffs out self-confidence. Negative people get negative results, so make the conscious decision to stop being negative.

Going There

I have talked about the Law of Attraction, but I really don't think it works in isolation. I believe there is a powerful spiritual element that pairs with the Law of Attraction to give you your greatest potential. I hope you aren't offended that I am daring to write about something that business writers and corporate speakers never talk about — the big taboo. But, spirituality matters, in good times and bad.

Whoa. I am going to "go there."

First, a caveat: I will never tell you *what* you should believe. I don't endorse any religion because I think all of them help us travel down different roads to get to the same place. I don't think any of us is more right than the other. I just hope you believe in *something.* Most people do. A 2008 study of more than 36,000 adult Americans found that 92 percent say they believe in God. It is the most extensive poll ever conducted on Americans and their religious beliefs, but other polls conducted by everyone from Harris to Fox News confirm the numbers.

If so many people believe, why is it considered so inappropriate to bring it up in a business context?

It's not – especially now.

Don't be afraid to "go there."

I am absolutely convinced that there is an energy out there that is bigger than any of us, and it is *big.*

I used to reserve my prayers for my most desperate moments, like when my mother had her stroke and it looked like she was going to die. Or when my father was shot in a holdup at his drugstore. I never wanted to bother God with things like career or finances – things I felt certain I should have been able to manage for myself. But when I couldn't get my first book published and I felt like an absolute failure, I did the only thing I could do: I prayed.

I didn't feel so alone.

Ever since, I have constantly counted my blessings and been rewarded with more abundance than I ever imagined and, best of all, a stronger spiritual connection. I never, ever feel alone or lonely. I always feel supported and loved.

There are so many people experiencing so many difficulties, and they come to me and I have no idea what to say. Is positive thinking the answer if you have lost your job and your house and you have a medical issue and no insurance – all at the same time?

What can you do when life gets that dark?

Have faith. Work the Law of Attraction, but do it in tandem with your spirituality. Believe in abundance and count on your spiritual connection to carry you through to the other side.

You may reserve prayer for the "really big issues" that confront you in life, and only make your spiritual connection in those moments when you think you are "supposed" to go to God. But, if you do that, you are closing yourself off from the deep bond that comes when you remain spiritually connected day-in, day-out. I count on that connection all the time. It's a partnership for me.

I used to think how ridiculous it was for football players to pray before a game. Why bother God with something like the score of a football game? But, I think we need to check in with God whenever we need help performing our best.

So, don't be afraid to "go there." What a wonderful thing to know that, regardless of what happens, you are being guarded and supported.

Control What You Say To Yourself

We are always talking to ourselves. We wake up in the morning and get ready for the day and decide quickly if it is a good hair day or a bad hair day. If we look fat or thin. For some reason, we are very eager to self-criticize, and we do it all the time. Why? What possible good can come from it? Yet, we invite self-negativity and give it unlimited air time in our brains. We will freely subject ourselves to a powerful barrage of nastiness, yet we'd never be so cruel to a stranger – or to someone we don't like. We are mean to ourselves, and we don't even see the damage we are inflicting.

Think about the negative things you have said to yourself in the last 24 hours. Just think of them! If someone said those things to your child, you'd want to scratch that person's eyes out. Yet, *you* are saying those terrible things to yourself – the one person you must love and care for above all others! Why do you stand for it? Do you realize that the tapes are rolling when you do this and those negative thoughts and feelings get stored on your internal hard drive to be played back ad nauseam? Those thoughts limit you in every possible way. Why are you putting them into your head?

It's time for an intervention. If you want a better life, you must take the easiest of baby steps to make it happen. All you have to do is figure out a few good things to say to yourself in order to get your mind to let go of the negativity.

I know the cynics will just roll their eyes and walk away at the mere suggestion of using affirmations to refocus and re-energize their lives, and that is fine. Let them. We'll just use them and go out and be happier and more successful. It's their choice to limit themselves.

Countless studies have proven the connection between positive affirmations (either through self-talk or hypnosis) and positive results. The concept is this: If you tell yourself you are attractive and fun to be around and repeat the thought enough times, your brain will overwrite your negative tapes that say you are unattractive and unworthy. You will come to believe you are attractive and fun to be around. Simple.

It works. Let's just say I am in one of my disorganized spells. I might say to myself, "I'm a mess. I can't get anything done, my desk is out of control and I can't focus." Well, what is the result? I can't get anything done and I can't focus. But, I can also launch into affirmation mode and repeat, "I am getting more organized by the minute. I am on task and producing better than ever." I might say it fifty times the first day, thirty times the second day, and so on. It doesn't take long for me to shift into high gear and start focusing hard and doing my work.

If you have your doubts of this positive self-talk programming, take a minute to examine what your negative self-talk has accomplished. I am sure it is significant.

Unfortunately, we humans are really mean to ourselves. We berate ourselves for gaining weight, failing in relationships, struggling at work, getting into tussles with family or not doing enough for the kids. We fail to let go of the inevitable criticism that comes our way through the years, remembering a kind word of praise for five minutes and a passing swipe until we die. We fixate on the few people who don't like us, rather than on the many who do. The list of sour thoughts that we put in our head and keep there goes on and on and on.

And, since we are sensitive beings, we don't just acknowledge our shortcomings, we revisit them again and again and again. We remind ourselves how we fall short – and we aren't even consciously doing it. We cling to nasty remarks that may have been said about us years ago – even decades ago – as though they were true and permanent. We joke about ourselves to others, but while those self-deprecating put-downs may be humorous, they serve to re-enforce our negative self-image.

And when it comes to body image? Hey, in my other books, I interviewed world renowned leaders who acknowledged horrible self-esteem problems that were rooted in what they weighed or how they looked. Few bothered trying to pretend their self-esteem was rock solid. The disease of our generation is self-loathing. We constantly beat ourselves up.

If we've failed at something, we remind ourselves of it long after we should have moved on. We tell ourselves we aren't smart enough or fast enough or credentialed enough to try something especially hard or new.

This is how we have *programmed* our thinking. We have put

all those dark thoughts in our head and repeated them so many times that they are the first thoughts we have when it comes to our performance, our place in the world and our self-worth. Write down ten negative things you have told yourself this week, and really look at them. Are they grounded in reality? Would other people say those things about you? Would they say it with such vitriol?

You are a flawed individual – just like everybody else. Big deal.

Don't be skeptical of the value of positive self-talk until you really look at the power and influence of all the negative self-talk with which you've filled your brain. Isn't it a wonder how some of us voluntarily tear ourselves down, telling us that we are so worthless and unattractive?

If you look in the mirror and see "fat," you will be fat. If you look at your career track and think "average," you will be average. If you look at possibility and see impossibility, you will encounter impossibility. You know it's true that when you say you can't, you can't.

So this book will, in part, teach you how to believe you can, because you can.

The beauty of it is, it is not hard at all to erase those negative tapes and overwrite them with positive ones that will drive you to a less stressful, more productive and happier life.

How It Works

The concept is very, very simple:

1. If you say something to yourself enough times, you will believe it.

2. If you write it down, it becomes real to your mind.

The downside is just as simple:

1.When you stop repeating those affirmations, they stop working.

2. When they stop working, the most strongly imbedded thoughts come back, and since you've been negative much longer than positive, those negative thoughts will come back.

And that means:

1. You have to be motivated enough to affirm yourself.

2. You have to do it, even when you don't feel like it.

Sometimes, it's not so easy. Seriously, repeating ten affirmations five times a day will take you what? Maybe two or three minutes total. But, when you are depressed and need self-affirming statements the most, it can be a real challenge to make yourself spend those few minutes reprogramming your brain to be kind to yourself.

The tapes inside your head are powerful. If you repeat a negative remark enough times, it will load itself onto the permanent memory of your personal internal hard drive. I don't believe you have the power to completely erase those tapes because it does seem like they are ready to play themselves again, as soon as you stop repeating your affirmations. But, you have great control over the tapes and possess the ability to write over the bad ones, recording positive, constructive and productive affirmations that your psyche will absorb and use if you repeat them enough.

Like I said, I am no different from anyone else. I have had good times and bad in this life. When I am in a bad spell, I have to remind myself how easy it is to fix things by saying the right words to myself. It's so easy, but it can be so hard to get started.

So, make up your mind. You want an easier way? You can

have it.

Pace Yourself

You don't lose fifty pounds in two weeks. You lose them one pound at a time. You don't begin a fitness regiment by running a marathon. You run a mile or two.

So don't stare at the prospect of de-stressing or rebuilding your life by expecting to change everything by midnight tonight. It's too intimidating. You are who you are. You may want changes, but those changes can't – and won't – happen in an instant.

The one thing I have seen repeatedly in people who face daunting challenges is that they often won't try because the situation seems too big and hard to conquer. They think they must do it all and fix it all – at once, and that's too hard so they just don't bother.

I once had a boss who went on a diet. And gave up smoking. And stopped drinking alcohol. And gave up coffee.

ALL AT ONCE!

Now, there might be a few hearty souls who might be able to handle that much life overhaul at once, but not many. Certainly not that woman, who morphed into the meanest, nastiest, foulest co-worker I have ever encountered. Within days, people were *begging* her to embrace her vices again – at least one or two of them.

And, of course, she did. In fact, she embraced them all. With fervor.

Twenty years later, she is still embracing them, although I think she mentioned a few months back that she'd quit smoking. I am just glad we live on opposite sides of the country.

The lesson here is that you have to mentally and physically position yourself for success – not failure. Even though I encourage you to test and push your limits as far as your imagination will let you, you still must do a reality check. You are a human being who can only do so much at once. Maybe you are the one-in-a-million mastermind who can leap tall buildings in a single bound, but if you can't, you might smash into the wall and give up altogether.

Really look at what you are up against and split the challenges into stages that you can knock off one or two at a time. I know that many of you feel like the obstacles have stacked up and must all be addressed at the same time. How do you deal with everything at once? You can't. Prioritize so you can do something rather than freezing up and doing nothing.

Make the decision – *really* make the decision, and plot out a way to make your immediate goals become reality. Once you have some momentum, you can add more to your list. And then, a little more. The more you do, the more you will be able to do at one time.

Don't fool yourself into thinking you have such superhuman stamina, willpower and determination that you can accomplish everything, all at once. But, don't use that reality to talk you out of striving for goals that seem out of reach. Again, it's pacing. Set a course that will push you and make you stretch, but don't set one that will kill you.

Pace yourself.

I once interviewed a man at a college graduation who started his studies back when he was a young father. It took him ten years to get that bachelor's degree! He did it one class at a time. It didn't matter what was going on in his life, he always had one class on his schedule to move him toward his ultimate goal. And, he achieved it.

You don't have to fix everything in one day. If you think you do, you will be tempted not to fix anything. Just take small steps.

I travel a lot for my speaking business and the thing I hate most is coming home to a dining room table covered with stacks of mail. I just can't deal with it, and so I leave it. Then the pile grows. And grows.

There came a point where there was not a single inch of space available on that table. One morning, I lamented this to a friend who told me, "Just set your timer and give it ten minutes of straightening time. You can do the same thing tomorrow. But, you only have to do it for ten minutes." Well, that didn't seem so bad, so I told myself I would do it.

I kept putting it off. Noon came and went, two o'clock, four o'clock, and finally I said to myself, "This is ridiculous. I only have to give it ten minutes." So, I set the clock, and focused on that table. Ten minutes later, I realized I was almost finished clearing it off entirely. It only would take another five minutes, which I gladly spent. Suddenly, that table was 100 percent clear of clutter.

It is exactly the same when trying to clear the clutter you have stacked up in your brain. Even if the outcome is peace of mind, inner strength and outright joy, the idea of changing your entire thought pattern, perceptions and attitudes sounds like work.

You don't have to change everything today.

You don't have to go into some twenty-three hour Zen zone of affirmation, affirmation to reprogram every negative thing about yourself.

Just give it ten minutes.

Just start.

Talk Yourself Into Succeeding

Sometimes we do hit the wall of our own limits, and some excuses do count. I want to sell ten million copies of this book, but I can't make ten million people buy it. All I can do is write the best book I can, and work like heck to promote it.

I may have wanted to win a Pulitzer Prize when I was a reporter, but all I could control was that I would do Pulitzer-quality work. I got four nominations, but never the prize.

If you want to act, you can't assure yourself that you will win an Academy Award. All you can do study, practice, and prepare yourself to perform at an Oscar-quality level.

If you want to be CEO of General Motors, you can only control that you have the knowledge, finesse and ability of someone who would ascend to that position.

You might want to do an Ironman Triathlon, but maybe your knees won't let you run at all.

Some excuses count. But again, not many.

For almost every challenge we encounter, there are a multitude of excuses that give us a pass to walk away. Maybe they make us feel less pressured, but excuses are just cop-outs for choosing that which appears easy over something that poses difficulty. Deep inside, we know that. But we use them anyhow.

We use excuses to talk ourselves out of trying for promotions we think we can't get. We use them to stay in jobs and relationships and circumstances that we don't even like. We use them to put off furthering our education, starting fitness programs, moving, losing weight, building relationships and doing those things that put us in our discomfort zones.

Excuses don't count. Results do. Stop talking yourself out of success.

Turn Off The Autopilot

I know a woman who began her second career as a Realtor when she was in her early 50s. She dove in, contacting all of her friends and asking all of us to pass her name on to all of our friends. She went through intensive training on cold-calling, then spent hours every day on the phone making those excruciating calls to strangers. She *had* to make a success of herself, and she did. Within three years, she was one of the top agents for one of the nation's largest real estate companies.

At that point, things got very easy. People came to her– she didn't have to go to them. The market heated up, then became red hot and her business expanded so quickly she could barely keep up with it. I could never reach her directly– she was that busy.

And then? Everything stopped. People stopped buying homes, she stopped making money and she confided a great sense of helplessness that made her feel defeated. She started living off her savings and lamented having to start a new career in her late 50s.

"Why are you giving in so quickly?" I asked.

"Real estate is dead."

"Dead?"

"Dead."

"You mean, dead as in *nobody* is buying homes?"

"Nobody is buying homes."

"Nobody? Not one home has sold in the last month?"

"Well, a few here and there."

"Because I look at the paper and they still have hundreds of real estate transactions listed here every week."

"Not me."

"*Somebody* is buying those homes and *somebody* is selling them."

"I haven't sold anything in three months. I'm not getting any clients."

"What have you done to attract them?"

"Postcards, ads and the usual."

"Cold calls?" I asked.

She grimaced.

"I stopped doing those years ago. They don't work very well."

"But, they worked well enough for you to start your business. Right?"

"Well…"

"When is the last time you reached out to your network and said you needed referrals and asked for help?"

"Everybody knows I am here now. I don't need to…"

"Are you making any money?"

"No."

"Then, you need to. You need to reconnect with your network, get the buy-in, ask everyone to start referring you to other people who will refer you to other people and until then, you get the joy of making some cold calls."

"That's for beginners. I am beyond that."

"It's for beginners who want to build their business. Don't be so impressed with yourself that you think you are too good to do the things that made you successful in the first place."

She grumbled a bit, but apparently, my coaching advice worked. We talked several weeks later and she'd gotten a few clients who were ready to buy. One of her friends even referred a transferring executive who called her one morning, rode around with her that one day, then bought a $600,000 house.

"I'd gotten smug," she admitted.

This is no time for being smug. We work so hard to make our name, then once we've got it, we look down our noses at the hard techniques that helped us succeed in the first place.

Stop Taking Your Work For Granted

When the economy goes south, you don't have to go with it. The best thing you can do to stabilize your situation is stop taking things for granted. Doing things the way you have always done them is often a bad strategy in a climate that is changing so rapidly. The status quo isn't working right now, so what can you do to deliver maximum performance and the greatest results?

That is not a question that can or should be answered quickly. Take time to look at what you do. If you or your company has seen dwindling results, deconstruct your assignments to see how you could escalate production, sales, contacts or whatever you are working with in order to, first, get things moving again and second, grow your business if possible.

This is the time when you must stop taking things for granted. Your success is completely dependent on your drive, ingenuity and initiative. Some people freeze up in times like these, but that is a big mistake. Things will get better, but when? Why would you wait things out if it could be a year, two years – or many more before cash starts flowing again?

Are you taking anything for granted? Have you gotten "too good" to do the heavy lifting that you once did? Do you need to start doing that heavy lifting again? Are there different strategies that might work to increase your output? What do newcomers in your business do in order to establish themselves? Should you try those things?

When my first book came out, I did signing after signing after signing at bookstores throughout Tampa Bay and Orlando. I spoke to any club – even at book clubs in people's houses. I not only sold books – I sold motivational T-shirts and burned my own motivational CDs on my home computer to sell and give me a little more income.

I was so hungry to succeed as a speaker that I drove for six hours to Miami for a pro-bono speech – and only twelve people showed! But, I had to get myself out there.

I was constantly trying to book radio and television interviews to get the word out. That eventually gave way to my own cold-call strategy where I would commit to contacting ten meeting planners every week – even if it killed me.

Now I don't do any of that. I know that I will sell hundreds of books at a single speech and keep all the profits, rather than selling a dozen books at a bookstore and get nothing. I know that the radio and television interviews are fun to do, but they eat up my time and don't help me book speeches, so I know I'd rather work on my marketing for a few hours in my office instead. I've got a formula that is working, and I am so glad because bookstore signings are grueling experiences.

I'm not taking anything for granted right now. I am just putting my energy where I will get the greatest payoff. That is what we all need to do. Really take a hard look at what will deliver the best results, then change your strategy to take advantage of those possibilities.

The minute my no-bookstore strategy stops working, you can bet I will revisit what got me going in the past. I love my work and I will be damned if the economy or anything else keeps me from doing it.

None of us can afford to be too stubborn or too proud to roll up our sleeves and re-establish ourselves. We can make this economy work *for* us, but *we* have to take responsibility for what we are doing and how we are doing it. We need to really analyze our behavior, decisions and actions to see where we can adjust our performance strategies so they deliver at the highest possible level.

Take Control

As we move along in our careers, there is a tendency to ease into auto-pilot and forget the kind of drive, commitment and tenacity we once had to possess in order to create our success. It is great that our success has shown us an easier way of doing things, but when things get hard, shut off the autopilot and take a few minutes to examine strategies for what you can do to kick-start your business again. It may well be that your old techniques do not work for your level of operation – but they might.

Truthfully, I don't think bookstore signings are going to generate more business for me, but I do think that, if things dried up, my old cold-call strategy to meeting planners would be a great way to direct my energy.

I was recently talking with another speaker who seemed to pity another major speaker who'd resorted to cold calling after losing a $300,000-a-year client. Well, I don't pity the speaker making those cold calls. I admire him. He's out there doing something. It's not a sign of desperation, but rather, commitment. Will a cold-call result in a $300,000-a-year client? I guess it could happen. It probably won't. But, those cold calls will result in *something*. And one thing leads to another. It keeps him from being a victim who is paralyzed by circumstance. I can't imagine losing a client that huge, but I'd be doing the same thing that guy is doing.

One thing I know is this: When I do nothing, nothing happens.

You don't slow down when your business slows down. You don't give up when your business suffers a major setback. Instead, you ratchet things up. You do that by examining all of the things that have worked to generate business for you in the past, and decide what will work for your future. Do that by looking at what has made you successful, and what has propelled your peers and competition. Evaluate and decide what will work for you. Do that by making up your mind that you are stronger than any adversity you encounter, and then get moving.

I am such a believer that our obstacles give us the greatest opportunities to define who we are as individuals. I say it every day: We have our greatest opportunity to succeed while everybody else is giving up. Don't give up. Be shrewd. Remember what got you where you are and tap into it. If you have let your career move on auto-pilot because things have worked well on their own, it is time to turn off the autopilot and take the wheel and steer for yourself. You did it in the past, and it worked. That gives you every reason to believe that you will be successful in the future.

How to Take Charge Again

1. Review your strategies. Spend a couple of hours revisiting the early days of your career. Write down a list of the strategies you used to make yourself successful. What worked? What didn't? What worked better? What are you doing now that you could refine to work better? Are there techniques you abandoned that might work now?

2. Connect with the right people. Have you done a good job staying in touch with the people who made a difference for you throughout your career? Not just the early contacts and mentors, but the people who helped you along the way? Who were your first customers or clients? Your first bosses? Make a list of the top 50 or 100 connections that helped you the most in the past 10 years. Examine the list closely and decide who you should reconnect with first, and how you will make your approach. An e-mail? Facebook? Lunch date? If people have helped you in the past, they will likely help you in the future. But, you need to *ask for help.*

3. Expend some energy. As hard as we work now, most of us can be honest and admit that we don't throw ourselves into the moment as forcefully as we did when we were first getting going. Back when you got started, it likely took you hours to do what you can now do in minutes, now that you "get" what you are doing. You might get so much more done these days, but remember the energy you had when you first got started. Let that inspire you again so you can recharge your efforts and take charge of the challenges you now face.

4. Understand your emotions. Now, spend a little time looking at where you are with your career emotionally. You may be extremely successful, but you may have lost some of the old fire that put you on the map in the first place. Write down the reasons you chose your career and what kept you in it. Decide that it is worth fighting for and recommit to it by falling in love with your work all over again.

Your Greatest Work of Fiction

Once you turn off the autopilot and start steering for yourself again, you'll need a plan that will be your action blueprint. Still, see your plan for what it is. A plan. It will get you moving and give you direction, but it will rarely come off without change.

I often joke about the initial plan I had for my life as an author. I was to write that first book in three months, then sell it for the high six figures, maybe seven. The book would then come out six months later, debuting on top of the *New York Times* best-seller list. Oprah would see the book on the shelves while out shopping at the Chicago Barnes and Noble, then buy it. She would love it so much that she would call me up in the middle of the night and have me whisked off to Chicago. I'd be there at her side as she'd tell the world to buy my book. She would so love me as an author that she'd in o much unexpected drama. I certainly never counted on that first book being rejected by every major publisher in America, or it being released a day before 9/11. I did not get a seven-figure advance and Oprah did not invite me to dinner with her and Steadman. However, I *did* get a best-seller (after real persistence) and did get my book on Oprah.

Have a plan, but plan to change it. Life will demand that you be flexible enough to make changes. The seemingly clear path you devise to turn your vision into reality will twist and turn and run into dead ends. It will lead you into brick walls and open fields. Things you expect to be hard might come very, very easy. Things you expect to come easy might never come at all.

A plan helps you refine your vision and gives you direction so you won't stall out. But, success does not happen according to plan. It happens, but you have to help it happen by being shrewd, quick-thinking and resolute about what you want. You can lament the twists and turns, or you can learn to expect them, and enjoy them for the extra challenges they present.

When my book kept getting rejected, I needed to know *why* it was being rejected. I had an old source from my reporting days whose son was an editor for a major publisher. I asked her if she could get him to look at my proposal and tell me what the problem was. She did, he did, and I ended up having to rewrite my whole book to make it more commercial. None of that was in the plan. I got the first copy on Sept. 10, 2001. The next day, our world collapsed. That led my publisher to cancel my tour and give up on me and my dream. I decided to go out there and fight for my book anyhow.

Since it had been *three years* since I'd had a job and I was financially operating on fumes, I plotted out my own tour that would let me stay in the homes of my friends all over the country. The cancelled tour was to take me on a glamorous route, flying me from New York to Boston to Los Angeles to Atlanta. I wound up traveling the country in a rented Ford Escort and eating off the dollar menu from fast food chains in places like Columbus, Ohio and Flint, Mich.

No glamour there, but it worked.

So, plans need tweaking as we go along. That's fine. It's another challenge that tests our commitment, resolve and drive. We're up to it. We just take nothing for granted.

Be The Go-To Person

I recently read one career expert's advice on how to survive in a climate where bosses are deciding who to keep and who to cut. The bottom line, this expert wrote, is that you have to kiss your boss' a**.

There may be some truth to that. But there is a way to be valued without selling out. Granted, this is not the time to go on a bitching crusade or start hurling insults at the person who makes sure your paycheck gets signed. Has the economy really changed the relationship we should have with our boss? Shouldn't we always be seen as low-maintenance and high-performance?

> **If you want to be treasured by your boss, be a treasure. It's pretty simple.**
>
> • *Make their job easier.*
> • *Hyper-perform and over deliver so they know they need you.*
> • *Make sure they know what you are doing.*
> • *Help your colleagues.*
> • *Volunteer for more work.*
> • *Build relationships with the key decision-makers.*

Shouldn't we always be recognized as "go-to" players who work well with others and help the whole team to deliver?

If you do all of that naturally, you won't have to suddenly start brown-nosing. You'll already be appreciated as somebody the company can't live without. The economy has nothing to do with it. Bosses like people who are easy to work with. They like people who make *their* jobs easier. They like people who are easy to have around.

That said, I know I have had many moments when I was not easy to have around because I was a change-agent, or a "mustang." That sometimes gave me the label of "trouble-maker." I had to write two books before I understood that, while that label is sometimes inevitable, it is not enviable and if you can find a way to be effective without it, you'll be way ahead of your peers. There is a way to be a tremendous contributor *and be* heard for your change-agent ideas without getting yourself labeled.

Enjoy the Moment

I often think of a story told to me by Kathryn Sullivan, the first American woman to walk in space. Her mission was to deploy the Hubble Telescope, and it entailed complicated, intricate steps that all had to be perfectly executed.

"This was not the time to be staring out the window. We had the professional futures of other folks and a lot of federal money placed in trust in our hands."

While she was doing her work outside the space shuttle,

Commander Bob Crippen called out to the astronauts and had them take a second to look away from their tasks "…so we would know this was not a training repetition in the safety tank. It was the real deal. There was a planet over our shoulders. He made us pause to absorb the reality, and I'm so glad he did. We could well have gone back in the airlock and said, 'Was that the training tank or was that for real?'"

When we immerse ourselves in so much intensity, it is so easy to lose perspective. The reward is not only surviving this madness or achieving our goals, but the joy that comes from trying to attain them. Which memory means most to you -- getting your college diploma, or remembering the things that happened on your way to earning it? Your wedding might have been a crown-jewel moment in your life, but wasn't it fun to go through all the giddiness of meeting and falling in love?

Remember that as you go on your way. Some of your challenges will be quite trying these days, but they provide you with a defining moment to live all out and be who you are. Enjoy that. The reward is in doing something different, pushing yourself, and feeling the support from your friends and family as you dare to be bold.

We can't really understand the power of perseverance until we have persevered through the darkest times. I can tell you to hang in there because things will get better, but until you've experienced your share of crucible moments, my words will ring hollow. Your greatest learning occurs when *you* walk through the fire and make it to the other side. It would be easier if you knew a) when you are going to prevail or b) *if* you are going to prevail. Unfortunately, once you start getting tested by obstacles, you seldom have a clue when or if there is going to be a payoff. All you can do is keep on keeping on. Or, you can quit.

Once you get to the other side of your difficulties – and you *will* get to the other side of your difficulties – you will have matured and learned and found a power within yourself that you never would have discovered if everything had unfolded with ease. Yes, these are challenging moments, but they are moments of great growth. That is a good thing. One day you will look back at all of this and see how these times shaped you and helped you grow. Hopefully, you will respect what you did to get through them.

So, as you turn off the autopilot and ratchet things up, enjoy the moment. You've got a real chance to prove what you are made of.

The Easy Way Is Usually Harder

If you are going to do something hard, you will encounter moments when you wonder why you are bothering. Why choose a difficult path when you can choose an easier route? That less stressful approach will always call to you if you haven't truly made up your mind, committed and continued to recommit on a daily basis.

Every day, remind yourself of what you are after and why you want it. Write these reasons down so that you can refer to them whenever you start thinking about letting go of your goals. It is so hard to maintain momentum when you encounter hurdles that you must get past, or even when you become bored.

There are often moments when you will see possible shortcuts as you try to accomplish your goals. But, shortcuts often prove to be the long way around an obstacle.

The only way to get through those tough moments is to continually remind yourself of what you are trying to accomplish – and why. It takes a firm commitment bolstered by consistent recommitment.

Success is easy when autopilot works. You don't have to do much besides show up and do what has been working all along.

But, millions of people are finding out that what used to work is not working anymore. You may need to look back at what generated business in the past. Or look at what other people are trying. Think big, think wild.

Don't look for an easy answer. Look for a strategy that will work.

Get Your Hands Dirty

I just finished speaking at a large event that was produced by one of the best teams in the business. It was the second time I had the privilege of working with these people and I was thrilled to see the stage manager. I asked her how business was going.

"It's scary," she said. "I keep getting notified about events that have been cancelled. It's one cancellation after another."

I told her to hang in there.

"When you asked me for my business card yesterday, it really hit me because I haven't even had business cards in years," she said. "I've moved two times since the last time I had cards. I didn't need cards because the business has always come to me…"

"And now you have to go find the business," I said. "You need cards."

"Yes. I took it all for granted," she said. "You said we have to work even harder and it makes me wonder if we've been kind of lazy all along. Is that it? I don't want to make calls, but every day I don't make a call, it is a day I am not going to get business."

"The rules have changed," I said. "The test right now is to be very, very busy and see what you can create for yourself. You'll be fine – but you've got to work it."

"Like I did when I started," she said.

Exactly.

Turn off the autopilot. It's time to really get to work.

Hyper-Perform

The greatest compliment I ever received for my work came when I met someone who told me, "You write the best weather stories I have ever read." I was well-known for my investigative reporting, but if I was writing good weather stories, it meant I was doing a good job with everything else. A good mentor taught me to write every story as if it were to be my last. My name was going on top of it. If I died after writing that one story – whether it was a blockbuster or an obituary – I wanted to make sure it was something for which I could be proud.

Imagine my shock when I became an editor and found that most of my people didn't bring that same degree of pride to work with them. I was stunned, not because they weren't like me, but rather, because they would submit stories filled with errors and problems. They wanted to go home and leave it to me to fix their work. They didn't care if those messes were printed in the paper and viewed by hundreds of thousands of people the next morning.

They didn't care that their names were going to go on top of that shoddy work. The whole world would know they didn't do a good job, but those reporters didn't care.

I was astounded.

Especially now, take pride in your work. Work may not be your whole reason for living, but you are being paid to be a contributor. Don't use your dissatisfaction with your paycheck, management or the uncertainty that abounds as excuses for delivering substandard work. Even if you are convinced you deserve better, you are where you are. There is not a lot of mobility in the current job force, so use this moment to perfect what you do and deliver your best possible output.

I know that is hard when everyone feels so demoralized. I look at people who are waiting to see who is going to be the next in line for cuts and wonder how anyone is capable of functioning, but function, we all must.

You must. Even if you are facing a loss of employment, you will be able to walk out the door knowing that *you* delivered. That you did not deserve to lose your job. That you gave it everything you had to give. Those are good things to know because that pride will propel you as you pick yourself up and position yourself to win again.

Stand Up And Deliver

It's really rough being a cheerleader for your company if you fear layoffs and budget cuts. If you think the place is going down, why kill yourself while you wait for the inevitable?

Well, a lot of good that attitude is doing you.

It doesn't matter how bad or good things are. Take pride in your work every single day and deliver your best because, more than ever, this country needs a strong, committed workforce at every level. If we are going rebound as a nation, we have to do it with our collective excellence.

Step up to the plate.

If you contribute your best, you help insulate your company and that, in turn, insulates you. Stellar performance on your part will give you the greatest degree of protection in case there are cutbacks or layoffs. Those who aren't the big contributors likely will be the first to suffer the ax. There are people who think it is best to keep their heads down and stay out of sight while those in power make decisions about changes or cuts, but that is a foolish strategy now. The deciders in upper management need to know you are working hard and making a difference every day. They need to see you as indispensable, not invisible.

We've all had times when we have managed to do the work of five people and accomplish more in a day, week, month or year than we ever thought possible. The brain and body are capable of operating in hyperdrive – but not indefinitely. If we force ourselves to do it all the time, we burn out. Yet, this is the moment when we must hyper-perform in order to contribute at a level that makes us most valuable and viable for our employers. This is a time when we must maintain our energy levels and find new ways to over deliver so that our work is noticed – and rewarded.

I've interviewed many corporate leaders faced with making cuts and this is really the bottom line: There is no room for average employees. If the average people aren't gone already, they will be. "Above average" workers? They are nice to have, but that's the next level to go. Outstanding people? They are becoming the workhorses of the labor force. And the hyper-performers who over deliver time and again? They are viewed as the key players who are creating the company's future.

What is "hyper-performance"? It is the kind of performance you deliver when you surprise even yourself by what you are capable of achieving. It is the exhausting level of delivery that stretches you and shows you that you are so much stronger, smarter, and faster than you ever knew. All of us can look back on our careers and see times when we really kicked some tail.

I remember the time I wrote a huge seven-day, 16-piece newspaper series in three days. My boss lavished me with praise and said, "Now that I know what you can do, I will expect this of you all the time."

I'd killed myself to do that series and, instead of him telling me how much he appreciated it and giving me time off to catch my breath, he told me that he'd raised the bar so I'd deliver at that level all the time.

Yeah, right.

But, seriously, we all know we can do more than what we are doing, even in those times when we don't know how we can squeeze any more out of our day.

THIS is the time to ratchet it up. THIS is the time to show how valuable you are. THIS is the time to shift into hyperdrive and deliver.

Work Smarter

Recent studies show that workers *admit* to losing between two and three hours *a day* to their own distractions. When AOL and Salary.com dug into it, they found that personal Internet use was the biggest problem. They surveyed more than 10,000 people, and nearly 45 percent blamed the Internet as their No.1 workplace distraction. I understand that because I stopped to check the Huffington Post while I was writing this paragraph. And, if I weren't trying to behave myself, I'd be checking my e-mail next.

The next big distraction was socializing with co-workers, which about a fourth of the respondents said was their worst attention pull.

After that, people reported they lost time to conducting personal business, flat-out "spacing out," running errands, making personal phone calls, job hunting elsewhere, planning personal events and arriving late and leaving early.

Now, if you are being honest, you've got to look at that list and see a little bit of yourself in it. I know I do. But, none of us can deliver our best work if we are surrendering to those kinds of work interruptions.

We've always been told to work smart. Now, we've got to work smarter. That means making our time matter more than it

Get It Done

Know your goals for the week and day. This keeps you focused and on track.

Amp up your to-do list. Structure your day for the tasks that will move you toward your goals.

Give yourself deadlines. Know how long each assignment should take, and try to complete it on schedule.

Declutter. Clean work spaces make it easier for you to be productive.

Stop procrastinating. Do hard or unpleasant tasks first.

Switch gears. If things aren't working out with what you are doing, either take a break or switch to another assignment and come back with a fresh mind.

Make your commute productive. Make calls. Do work or read when you are on mass transit.

Meet smart. Have an agenda, and send it around before the meeting. If you have a choice, use it to decide which meetings you will attend. Handle what you can in e-mails and conference calls, but when you meet, don't let things drag on endlessly.

Delegate. Don't be proud or stupid about doing what other people are able to do. You don't have to do it all, you just have to see that it gets done right.

Return phone calls during lunch. Leave a voice message, that way you spend one minute connecting, not ten.

Keep it in perspective. Few will keep tabs on which meetings you missed, but your children and spouse won't forget. It doesn't matter what the economy does. Family first.

ever has. We've got a million opportunities to distract ourselves, but we will never get anything done if we spend our work lives scouring eBay.

Get it together. Really look at your distractions and devise a method for minimizing their pull on you.

First, know what it is that you have got to do. It is amazing how many people go through the day thinking, "Well, I've got to do this and this and that, and some of this and some of that," but never step away from their to-do list long enough to figure out what their actual goals are. If you want to get the most out of your time and focus, then I suggest you begin by having goals set for each week and each day. If, on Monday, you know you have to do x, y and z during the week, you aren't going to get lost in your out-of-control to-do list. Goals and tasks are not the same thing. Your goals will keep you in check, because they help you to manage yourself toward an accomplishment.

Write down the tasks you need to accomplish in order to achieve your goals, then put them on your to-do list. Before you leave work at night, write down your goals and tasks for the next day.

Some people accomplish more by breaking their lists down into time blocks with a specific amount of time allotted to each task. That's not such a bad idea, because it gives you three advantages. First, it keeps you from meandering through or wasting your day because you have some mini-deadlines to keep you in check. Second, it lets you take a real look at when you are most productive and schedule your hardest work for that time. Third, it keeps you from procrastinating. You know what you need to do and when you need to do it.

Figure out what you need to do and consciously plan how you are going to do it. It is amazing how simple it is to put yourself on track if you can just focus for a few hours.

Hyper-Performance v. Workaholism

Please don't confuse the notion of hyper-performance with workaholism. Those are two different beasts. You want the first one – not the second.

Hyper-performance means you put performance first while you work. Workaholism means you put work first, period. It is not admirable, desirable or even healthy to choose that weary path. If you have been doing that all along, find a healthier way to be effective in your job. You'll live your life and then die. And, what will it all have been for?

You can accomplish just as much in the hyper-performance mode and still have time to have a life. In fact, you can't perform at this level long without some sort of balance. If you can leave work and leave it behind, you can come back to it renewed.

I just led a panel with senior executives who all said they don't want people in significant decision-making positions if they are chained to their work, day and night. Workaholics don't bring fresh energy to the office. They lose perspective.

So, don't use this downturn as an excuse to become a one-dimensional, work-first kind of person. The workaholics are an interesting breed, and some of them do pretty phenomenal things. But, as a whole, I have noticed that workaholics are often less productive than the people who work smart, not long.

To be a great hyper-performer, you need to make up your mind that you want to deliver at the highest level, then brainstorm the ways you can do it. What can you do to make yourself most valuable to your company? In most cases, the answer is to use your brain – all of it – in a focused and determined manner. That doesn't mean you sacrifice your home life and any outside activities, becoming a pathetic drone who eats, drinks and breathes his or her job. You do not have to do that. This is all about using your brain, working hard and getting results by being focused.

If you have a family, it is especially essential that you are there for your family members because these times take their toll on everybody. And, what matters most? Obviously, your paycheck matters a great deal. But, your presence is just as important. You don't have to sacrifice that in order to hyper-perform at the office.

Make Your Luck

One summer, I happened to be camping at Cumberland Island National Seashore in Georgia when a hurricane came up the coast. I was still a reporter then, and I went with the park rangers as they raced to evacuate the island, and grabbed a boat back to the mainland before the storm hit. The resulting front-page stories were dramatic, exciting, and all mine.

"Lucky Fawn," snarled a reporter who sat near me.

A few years later, I wrapped up a ten-month investigative project that toppled a huge portion of city government in Denver. Those ten months were brutal: The people I wrote about held press conferences to try to discredit my reporting. Officials demanded meetings with my editors and the publisher to insist I be yanked from the story. But, my stories were spot-on accurate. I was more stressed and exhausted than I'd ever been. Since I knew I was right, I kept fighting.

Everything climaxed one week with an announcement by the Colorado Attorney General and the Internal Revenue Service that they were investigating the people I was writing about. There were some very public firings, and ultimately, laws were changed because of those stories. The day of the firings, I went back to the office to write the story. My desk mate patted me on the back.

"You are so lucky," he said. "I keep waiting for someone to give me a story like that."

I didn't know what to say. Nobody *gives* you a story like that. You get a tip and you bite into it and run around like an obsessed bounty hunter until you nail everything down. You run a story, bite into the next part of it and do the whole thing all over again. And again and again until you really have it.

Was it luck that put me on that island at the time a hurricane came up the coast? Maybe, but luck didn't make me pull out a notebook and start reporting that story. The very morning of that hurricane, a handful of reporters met in the newspaper parking lot and carpooled to a river to go tubing down a favorite Florida river. When they got back to their cars, they found notes on their windshields asking them to report to the city desk and help with storm coverage. No one did it. They said they thought it was a joke. One of the reporters who skipped out was the woman who seemed so jealous of my big story.

Luck may put you in the right place for opportunity, but you've got to run with it. You don't get what you don't go for, and if you go for something halfway, you'll get a mediocre result. You want to hit the ball out of the park, you have to swing at it, and you have to swing hard, deliberate and with confident aim.

Look around your office. It's all the same thing. Some people produce because they are hell-bent on producing. And, some people don't produce. There are always excuses, but it is so true: Excuses don't count. Results do.

Are you taking advantage of every opportunity that comes by you? Are you actively looking for chances to stretch and hyper-perform?

Overpower Your Slumps

Obviously, some people don't drink the optimism Kool-Aid® and the notion of "hyper-performance" goes way beyond the pale. They are so down in the dumps over the doom-and-gloom climate that they'd be happy if they could find the energy to just get back in the game and perform a little. But, they can't.

They're in a slump.

We've all had times of remarkable productivity followed by inertia slumps where we can't get anything done. What was it they used to say? "When you're hot, you're hot. When you're not, you're not."

Over the years, there have been plenty of spells when I was *not* hot. Or warm. Or even lukewarm. My performance was excruciatingly cold. And, I wish I could write this chapter with full confidence that my slumps are behind me, but I know there will be more performance slumps in my future.

Fortunately, I learned from experience that a good slump is really a much-needed brain vacation. The last one came two years ago, after I'd spent six years burning myself out. My brain needed a break, so it took one.

If it weren't for my extensive experience falling into and climbing out of slumps, I might have worried. But, I looked at my situation. Remember that. Brains need breaks.

Bosses label those spells when we shut down or slide from excellence into mediocrity as slumps. I see my slumps as a way to take time to recharge my batteries so I can perform again. It took a lot of years for me to learn that I can't drive in fifth gear every day without completely burning out. And, I remembered that when I became a manager and saw my people go through the same experience.

We do not have an inexhaustible supply of energy; we have limits. Success comes in cycles. It is never a straight shot from earth into the stratosphere, so when you catch yourself sliding a little, don't panic. It has happened to everyone.

So, don't be depressed if you've fallen into your own personal downturn. But, get back in the game – *now.* Again, if you aren't delivering your best work, you are vulnerable in the current work environment. Even though slumps are common and inevitable, this is not the time to indulge a long personal work siesta.

There are a few things you can do to take charge over the situation. Since this is the time when you *must* at least deliver – if not *over* deliver – I want to help you to stop wallowing and start performing.

Take Charge Of Your Performance

If you spend too much time worrying about your lackluster performance, you will create even more mediocrity. Keep your eyes open. Know when you are in a slump, but feel certain that you will have the ability to get out of it and redeem yourself to the universe.

Worry and negativity puts you in a dark loop that will drag you down so much deeper than you need to go, thus increasing the pressure on you and making it even harder to get moving. You can make a slump as long or as short as you want. I, of course, suggest you make it short.

Time has taught me that I may not be able to control the onset of a slump, but I do have some control over its duration. That doesn't mean I can go from doing nothing to doing everything by clicking my ruby slippers together three times and telling myself I am on fire again. It does mean that I can organize myself so I can get some momentum – any momentum – by writing down lists of the things I have to do in order to get moving again. I put everything on the list. EVERYTHING. And then I make a time commitment to hard work – for a limited period.

For example, I'll say "I am going to work hard for two hours today." And that might not seem like much, but it is a lot when you aren't really working at all. So then I will start checking off those tasks on my list. If I can go for more than two hours, great. But, I have to do at least two.

The next day, three.

The day after that, four.

Reprogram your self-talk so that, instead of telling yourself "I suck and can't get anything done," you tell yourself "I am more productive every day and am very proud of my work." Instead of holding yourself down by saying, "I'm not performing, I am failing and I will probably get fired," tell yourself, "I know what I am doing and I do it enthusiastically." Say your positive affirmations fifty times a day if you have to. Soon, they will take hold and your performance will begin a swift rebound.

Combining the list mastery and positive self-talk usually will work. But, don't beat yourself up when you fall short. Can you imagine a batter being able to hit three home runs in *every* ballgame? Imagine the pressure for that guy, when he gets nine million dollars a year and can't even get a hit? We all want to be able to deliver every single time, but we aren't made that way.

Just remember to take the steps that will lift you out of your inertia and position yourself to hyper-perform once again.

Advertise Yourself

If you are waiting for other people to notice and reward your good work, you are making a huge mistake. Bosses are mostly worried about two things: 1) Themselves 2) The problems they have to deal with.

Although many are good at acknowledging good work, few spend time making lists of the good things their people are doing. Even fewer are actively passing on all that good news to their superiors. Your boss might have an idea how critical your contribution is, but his or her boss probably does not.

If you think it is enough to just do a good job, assume it is not. If you think others will notice and remember when you have accomplished something, assume they won't. If you think that, come promotion time, all of the supervisors will have memorized all the reasons you are so qualified, assume they haven't.

If you want more than you have, you have to promote and

position yourself for more. That means you should do everything from dressing at least one pay-grade better than your peers to taking on assignments that will make you more visible. You consistently should share your successes and achievements with your superiors in writing and act like the professional you want others to see.

I know some of us hate the term, "self-promotion" almost as much as the concept. One executive told me, "I prefer to say I am 'advertising my skills.'" Regardless of what you call it, you've got to do it if you want more for yourself. Your boss and your boss' boss and other senior leaders need to know what you know and what you do if you want to be considered for advancement.

While you do this, make your intentions known. Let the decision-makers know that you are serious about advancing your career. Some people do that by making appointments with people in power and frankly stating their goals and objectives. They might ask what might be done to help them to achieve their goals and move up the ladder. They might press for timetables and follow-up meetings. And, depending on the personality of the individual workplace and the individuals in charge, that strategy might work very well. Then again, it might not. You'll know best by assessing what other fast-trackers have done that has worked at your company.

Own The Game

There is so much opportunity out there if you just make up your mind to seize it. That means working hard now – harder than you have ever worked. Stand up, stand out. Deliver. Over deliver. If you are a constant example of contribution and excellence, you will rise above this adversity, either at your current place of employment or the next.

I know it is hard to project exuberance when it feels like your feet are sinking in quicksand. But, your attitude will change your world – if you let it. Consciously decide to be a player, then play. Play hard. Do your very best on everything you do. Have pride in your work and pride in yourself.

These are moments of great self-definition. When we get beyond these tough times and you look back at how you made it through them, are you going to see yourself as someone who showed courage or fear? It's your choice.

The Sky Is NOT Falling

I was hiking in the mountains near Telluride, in Southwest Colorado. It was summer – wildflower season – and, halfway into the trek, the thunderclouds arrived. I was alone, and I knew those clouds meant an almost-certain drenching. I'd forgotten my jacket.

I walked faster, harder – so hurried that I didn't dare to stop or slow down to look at the scenery. I had to get back. I knew I was going to get caught out there, and I'd get soaked, for sure. I started obsessing about lightning. I had to get off that mountain.

So much of the mountain was wide open and I was completely exposed at the highest point around. How was I going to protect myself? Nobody knew where I was. What if I got hurt? I wished my cell phone would work, but I was in a dead zone. It was just me.

I remember getting back to my car in the parking lot. The storm never even broke. The mountain was as undisturbed as ever, and I was more exhausted from the stress I'd brought upon myself than I was from rushing the trail. Not one drop of rain. Not a single crack of lightning.

How often have you done that? Not just when you are outdoors, but when you are anticipating an impending storm that never materializes. We all need to keep our eyes open for potential trouble, but we don't need to obsess over clouds that may never deliver the first drop of rain.

The media are more than happy to warn you that the dark clouds are hovering right over your head these days, ready to drench your safe little world. Maybe you should carry an umbrella, but don't worry yourself out of living. You can spend your life trying to avoid the storms or you can keep on trekking, certain you will be okay – no matter what.

Besides, a little rain never hurt anybody.

It is true that there are many, many pitfalls these days. You may be wondering how you will make your mortgage, what you are going to do about your job or career, how you will ever recover the money from your portfolio or any number of worries.

Does worry really help?

Sometimes we manifest dark results without experiencing dark realities. Your worry only will fill your life with stress and zap your life of the joy that comes by facing life as it comes.

What were you worrying about a year ago today? Two years ago? Can you even remember? And, how many of those fears actually came to pass? We get so tied up in our worries that we lose perspective that most of what we fear never even happens. The storm never comes. Still, we stare at those clouds endlessly, fearing them, trying to outrun them.

There is a "sky is falling" mentality for situations and complications that never manifest themselves in reality. Why do we do that? Do we have to?

I'm not saying you should ignore potential trouble spots and refuse to plan for action until something actually happens. Some problems can't be avoided. But, don't obsess about your worries. Assess them. Decide how real the threats are. Come up with a plan of action, but don't fixate on the negatives. Just do what you need to do and take steps to continue enjoying your life. Know you are ready to do what you need to do *if* you need to take action, but you have the power to live your life in as much peace as possible. Make the decision to consciously put worry in its place.

At least 95 percent of the things I have worried about never even happened. My obstacles and setbacks were rarely on my list of worries, but I dealt with them and everything worked out.

If most of your worries will never become reality, why give so much energy to them? Why not take charge over that thought process and steer yourself toward a calmer, more productive way of thinking and living?

Take A Worry Breather

What did Scarlett O'Hara do in *Gone with the Wind* whenever her problems seemed too great? She'd say, "I can't think about that right now. If I do, I'll go crazy. I'll think about that tomorrow."

There are times when stress piles up and all you can really do to fix it is pull a Scarlett.

Just delay the worry, go into denial and maybe it will go away. Granted, if your house is burning down, you'd better turn on a hose. But, there are so many situations where you can find your strength by delaying your worry. Given a little time and perspective, things rarely seem as bad as when you first confront them.

After you have taken that breather, use affirmations to put the situation in its proper place. You are in charge, not the worry.

> ## Affirmations to Reduce Your Worries
>
> • *I approach life with a carefree and can-do attitude.*
>
> • *I choose what I worry about and keep my worries in perspective.*
>
> • *I don't bother myself with things that may or may not happen.*
>
> • *The only thing on my plate today is today.*
>
> • *I choose to live my life rather than worry myself to death.*
>
> • *The better I get at letting things slide, the healthier and happier I will be.*
>
> • *I am smart, capable and have good support. I can handle whatever comes up.*

The situation won't kill you, but the stress-induced heart attack from the worry might. Scarlett O'Hara mastered the technique of silencing the "monkey mind."

Do you have a "monkey mind"?

I sure do.

Monkey mind is a Buddhist concept. It is the idea that some of us are so trapped in our worrying heads that our thoughts jump from one thought to the next in the same way that a monkey jumps from tree to tree. Since we are never really present, we lose sight of reality. Here is a thought map of how it works:

"I'm really struggling... Everyone is losing their jobs, I wonder if I'll lose mine...If I lose my job, I'll lose my house...How will my family survive all of this...None of this is fair...It is so hard...I don't know what else I can do...I worked too hard for any of this to happen...I can't believe what has happened to my investments...I'll never dig my way out of this..."

Then, your monkey mind starts right back over at the top of that thought map, putting more of the same garbage into your head. Your brain can really do a number on you – if you let it. Or, you can make it work for you.

One thing you have to do is get a grasp on reality. So many people are so frightened right now that they are gripped by a doomsday kind of fear that makes them expect the very worst out of every possibility. If bad things are happening to others, they figure bad things are bound to happen to them.

It is easy to understand how we slip into that kind of thinking because it comes down to basic brain function.

You can reprogram your monkey mind to stop the endless negativity loops and replace the dark thoughts with thoughts like these:

1. I've really got it together in this situation.

2. I am strong and resilient.

3. I feel courage – not fear.

4. When all is said and done, I will make so much money in this situation.

5. I feel more confident than I have ever felt.

6. I am stronger every single day.

7. I am learning so much about myself in this process.

8. Everything is going to work out just fine.

9. I can handle anything.

It takes work. The way the Buddhists control the monkey mind is through calming breathing exercises. The simplest one is to take a breath and, while inhaling, tell yourself, "I am breathing in." While exhaling, tell yourself, "I am breathing out." Do that for a few minutes and focus on the breathing. Pretty soon, the monkey mind shuts itself down. You've moved back into the present moment, where all that matters is your breath.

This is a great way to stop your brain from sliding into the catastrophic mindset that will cripple you and darken your future. Calm down. Center yourself.

What Is The Worst Thing That Can Happen?

Certainly, there are millions of people experiencing unprecedented hardship and facing choices they never thought they'd have to make. I doubt any of the people in foreclosure bought their homes expecting to hand them back to the bank, yet that's what happened.

Is a foreclosure the worst thing that can happen? A bankruptcy? A foreclosure *plus* a layoff?

All of those situations are pretty bad, but look at what you have in your life. If you are still healthy, you've got something that a lot of people would love to have.

Years ago, I visited the Grand Canyon with a forever friend who had been diagnosed with breast cancer at age 35. We were sitting around and I was lamenting how much weight I'd gained, telling her how bad I felt about myself and how it pained me to look in the mirror.

"Gee, Fawn," she said. "You're healthy. I'd love to have your body."

That really shut me up.

Sometimes we have it bad – really bad – but it isn't that bad when we put things in perspective.

Another woman described to me the suffocation she experienced when she was drowning in bills and credit card debt she could not handle.

"I was getting dunned, which means they are calling you all the time to ask you when you are going to make some arrangements. Finally, I said, 'Okay, I'm going to give you my address so the police can come and arrest me. You're going to have to take me to jail. There is no way I can pay this down.'"

She'd been making payments of upwards of $400 a month on an $18,000 consolidated credit card debt, and she'd paid off the original amount at least once, if not twice. She missed a single payment when she was on vacation, and that changed her interest rate and service charges and this and that and, suddenly, she was told she owed $27,000.

She couldn't keep up.

The guy sympathized with her and said, "I've been there, too." He told her to get a lawyer and file for bankruptcy. She got a lawyer and, after a five-minute hearing in bankruptcy court, her debt went away.

She never wanted a bankruptcy in her life. "It was about my good old American ethics," she said. "I'd made those charges. When you are a straight-up citizen type, you don't want to see yourself as a welsher."

But, she realized bankruptcy was her way out of the stress that she could not otherwise fix. She filed. She went to court. She was bankrupt.

How did it feel?

"It felt wonderful! It felt just fine! I felt, 'Thank goodness I am out from under that.' It was very nice not to be getting the telephone calls or worry about those payments. The world did not end."

If you are hanging on for dear life, there may come a point when you just have to let go.

What is the worst thing that can happen? The answer to that is different for all of us. I think the worst thing, for me, is watching someone I love suffer.

Know what the real "worst" thing is for you, and then put your current situation in perspective. You'll get through it. Liberate yourself by letting go of your fears.

If you are terrified of a looming foreclosure, I certainly understand that. But, if that happens, will you be living on the streets? No. There are plenty of landlords out there who are desperate for renters. The last time I ran an ad for one of my houses, thirteen of the fifteen families that checked out the house were fresh out of a foreclosure or bankruptcy. You are not alone in this. Almost all of the people in foreclosure admitted they felt some relief to finally have the nightmare over. They said they held on for dear life, doing everything they could to prevent that foreclosure. Foreclosure was the worst-case scenario, but once they finally let it happen, they were free. There was no more worry about it. It was done.

The sky is not falling. You can only know that if you have a real sense of what the worst-case scenario is for you?

Putting It In Perspective

1. What is the worst thing that can happen?

2. Seriously, is that the *worst* thing that can happen?

3. If most of the things we worry about never happen, why do we spend so much time worrying?

4. Have you taken steps to shut down the "monkey mind" negativity that is making things seem worse than they are?

5. Have you spent time counting your blessings so you know the goodness that still exists in your life?

6. Remind yourself that you are smart and strong enough to deal with anything.

7. Look around you. You are not the only person experiencing these difficulties.

8. You'll get through it. Pride is no longer an

issue.

Sometimes, I see myself back on that mountain. I see the clouds in the distance and know they may mean trouble, but then again, maybe not. I like the shadows they cast on the hills. They are beautiful. I watch them, not sure whether they will threaten me or not, but I know I am okay. Rain or no rain, I am okay.

Lead, Follow Or Get Out Of The Way

More than 200 years ago, Thomas Paine told his compatriots to "Lead, follow or get out of the way." Those words are spot-on today. This is no time to be in the way. You either lead or follow. This is no time to be an obstructionist. There is too much to do.

Some people react to turmoil by climbing into a hole and keeping their heads as low as they possibly can. That may seem like a good strategy for self-preservation, but it really is a bad idea. Those who are invisible are expendable. Those who have the courage to stand up and be part of the solution are seen as the go-to players who will save the day.

This is no time to blend in. It is a time to reach inside yourself and decide if you are bold enough to stand up and make a difference. If you can't lead, then be one hell of a follower, working hard to bolster your leader's success. But, don't limit yourself. This is such a great time to define your potential by taking risks, brainstorming solutions and delivering with follow-through.

Times have gotten tougher, but so have we. Ten years from now, you will be able to look back on these days and see people you know who emerged with incredible success because they stepped up and made the significant contributions that helped turn things around. This is your greatest moment to see how you can be one of the standout people who pitched in and made a difference.

There are chain-of-command and office political dynamics that may interfere with your ability to gain position to make change, but figure those things out. Make the connections you need to make by being visible, volunteering for extra assignments, and being a positive force with ideas and energy.

First, you have to stop focusing on how difficult everything is, about how much times have changed and about how bad it is out there. *This is your moment.* This is your greatest opportunity to step forward and demonstrate what you are made of. Your brilliance is needed, so figure out what you have to offer and position yourself to offer it.

Seeing Yourself As A Leader

Why is it that we assume that people who get to the top and become CEOs or senior executives have some sort of special DNA that makes them more capable of doing great things than the rest of us? There is no special leadership DNA. No success microchip. I have interviewed so many "super leaders" who readily admit that the only thing that separates them from the rest of us is that they dare to bet on themselves and work like hell to make sure they succeed. Sure, they know they are smart. They also see a world of untapped brilliance below them because so many workers are afraid to operate at the highest levels.

Guess what? You are probably smart enough to be a senior executive. Whether you are bold enough is up to you.

Are the super-leaders different from us? Smarter? More adept? In some cases, they are. There are always people who

Gaining Ground While Others Lose Hold

•*Have you made a conscious decision to get in front of these challenges and be a player?*

•*What are your greatest strengths? What can you contribute?*

•*Are you viewed as a "go-to" person? If so, are you delivering the goods? If not, what do you need to change?*

•*If you were the big boss, what would you change to make the company more successful during tough times?*

•*How can you stretch beyond your defined role to take an active role in the solutions process?*

•*Do you have access to the people who can help you implement some of the ideas you have?*

• *If not, how will you expand your network to include those people?*

•*How can you best communicate your thoughts and ideas without being shut down?*

•*Are you working hard enough?*

are smarter and more savvy than we are. There are people who have more talent, ingenuity and better instincts. There's always someone who knows more. You can either see that and quit right where you are, or see the strengths you possess and make the decision to use what you've got and go for broke. You don't have to know everything. You just need to know *enough*.

I once covered the mayor of a large metropolitan city who posed an especially difficult challenge to local cable crews covering city council meetings because he could not stop picking his nose – not even when the camera was right on him. His grammar was terrible and he sounded like a hick. Those of us in the press made jokes about him, but he led that city into an era of greatness it had never experienced before or since. He was visionary and capable, and he made himself a tremendous success – despite his very obvious shortcomings. He wasn't a hick. He was a man who wasn't afraid to put himself out there, flaws and all.

I know he heard people telling him that he was not polished enough for a career in politics, or that he didn't have the finesse or savvy to engender the support he would need in order to drive the kinds of change such a radical vision demanded. But he just went about his business. He created his own greatness.

We have all heard compelling stories of people who have risen from hard knocks to achieve unthinkable success. Remember Bill Clinton's horrible and humble beginnings, growing up in a poor home with a physically abusive stepfather? Or Oprah Winfrey, who grew up impoverished and sexually abused? Is there any need to make a list like this? The greatest success stories are everyday occurrences, like when some kid, fresh out of high school, makes his first million, or an immigrant comes to this country speaking no English but overcomes the language barrier and makes his fortune. Are those stories about the smartest people in the world? The most educated people? People who were tapped by some Grand Poobah or Great Pumpkin for special greatness?

No. Those stories are the inevitable byproduct of what happens when people are courageous enough to believe opportunity exists for everyone who has the guts to grab it.

There is no leadership DNA! There is no success microchip! You've got all you need to play in the big leagues.

You know enough to do more than you are doing. You know enough to manage more than you are managing. You know enough to influence more than you are influencing. You know enough to achieve more than you are achieving. Until you realize that you do know "enough," you will limit your advancement and reserve the greatest opportunities and the best jobs for other people who are not holding themselves back.

If you think you are fairly confident and accomplished, ask yourself if you have given enough thought to advancing upward. Do you see yourself running your company? You may not have the desire or drive. But don't talk yourself out of senior leadership because you think that status is reserved for someone who has that invisible special something that you don't think you have. The only "special something" that great leaders have is *nerve*. There is a switch inside the brain that says "go for it." Great leaders have the nerve to turn it on and the drive to succeed.

You may tell yourself that you are happy with your mid-level salary, that you already have accomplished more than you ever expected to accomplish and that things are just great the way they are. That spares you the headaches of going into foreign territories, having to learn new things and prove yourself all over again. If you feel comfortable, why shake it up?

There *is* great peace of mind when you feel good about the life you have made for yourself. But, there is so much excitement when you try new things and challenge yourself – particularly in a challenging time like this. There is so much you can accomplish now, so what is holding you back?

Why Not You?

I've noticed that people working at mid-level jobs seem to work about the same number of hours as people who work up in the executive offices. Sometimes, they work even more. So, if you are going to work hard no matter where you work, and you are going to work the same number of hours, why cheat yourself out of some great chances to advance, make more money, do different things and have a good time? If there is any part of you that thinks, "That'd be so cool, but I don't think I'm up to it," stop holding yourself back and just make up your mind that this is your moment to step forward, try new things and exert a greater influence.

I know that many people *absolutely do not want* the headaches of senior leadership, and that is their decision to make. In fact, if I were in the corporate world, I might make that same choice. But, don't make that decision based on the misguided assumption that you are not cut out for more. It is rare for me to see individuals who are performing at their maximum level of competency. If you can ratchet things up a bit, why not try it?

Looking Up

•What assumptions have you made about the people in senior leadership positions around you?

•Have you held yourself back by seeing limits, rather than possibilities?

•What skills do senior leaders have that you have? What do you think you are lacking?

•What can you do to expand your skills base so you can operate at that level?

•Are there operational areas where you need to work in order to get the expertise to lead at a higher level? Even if it involves a lateral transfer (or slight demotion), will it be worth it to get the knowledge you will need in your skills bank?

•Do you have the right connections with people two or three levels above you so they can see you in positions of greater authority? How can you expand your network?

•Do you see opportunities to gain visibility and expand your influence? Are there opportunities to fill any gaps that are not being handled?

So many people cut themselves off from advancement opportunities because they are convinced they don't know enough to do the job. You don't need to know specifics for most leadership jobs, you need to know leadership. You need to have vision and direction, and need to rely on good people who know what you don't know.

Leadership means having vision, surrounding yourself with good people, and then having faith in them to help you fill in the blanks you can't fill in for yourself.

I have interviewed so many successful leaders who have never known more than the basics of their "specialties," yet turned in phenomenal results because they relied on their people to handle that which was out of their grasp. Why should the CEO know every detail? They hire other people to worry about details. The CEO is responsible for overall direction.

You are as remarkable as you allow yourself to be.

Stand. Up. And. Lead.

It's easy to lose sight of this basic truth when, in one news cycle, one company is laying off 40,000 people and another is cutting 50,000.

Just remember this: You matter.

What and how you contribute at work matters more today than it ever has. Companies and co-workers are desperate for good leadership and innovation to carry them out of the chaos.

You can fixate on the possibility that your job will be eliminated and this or that horrible thing will happen to you and your family, or you can make up your mind that you are going to move out in front of the situation and do something that will help your colleagues, your company and your spirits.

Stand Up And Lead

It doesn't matter whether your title is CEO or administrative assistant. Stand. Up. And. Lead. This is no time to blend in. *Lead.*

I saw a great example of it the other day when I was crossing the street in Chicago with about fifty other people who ignored the flashing "DO NOT WALK" sign. A crossing guard held up a sign and commanded "You all GET BACK! You do NOT cross now!" She wasn't screaming. Her volume was just enough to be heard, but her essence was so powerful that all of us shifted right back in reverse, quickly walking backward to the curb and waiting for permission to cross again.

> ## Find opportunities to volunteer to do more.
>
> *Some questions for you to ponder:*
>
> •*Which areas are handled well already?*
>
> •*What needs extra support?*
>
> •*Do you have any original ideas that might fix an existing problem?*
>
> •*Are there any of the difficulty areas on your list that you can take over and own for yourself?*
>
> •*What is your best way of volunteering for extra work?*
>
> •*What do you need to do to show that you have adequately processed what needs to be done and come up with a workable strategy?*
>
> •*To whom do you need to communicate these ideas?*

Believe me, if she were running a corporation, people would listen to her.

Don't confuse leadership with management. Management is all about the boss/subordinate relationship. Managers need to be good leaders, but leaders operate at all levels of a company and all around us. If ever there was a time for you to stand up and show the world what you are made of, this is it. Your attitude, ideas, input, energy, support and encouragement can propel and inspire others at a time when they don't feel compelled to do much of anything.

Don't be distracted by internal bad news, horrible financial forecasts or gossip of impending doom. Focus on contribution. Until the very last moment, focus on what you can do to contribute to your company and your colleagues – *then deliver.*

The greatest leaders in history all emerged during times of strife and adversity, in times when people were desperate for someone to stand up and show them the way. There is so much opportunity right now, but few people see it and even fewer seize it. Instead, they seek cover, holding onto whatever security they think they have and hoping that things will just work out.

They wait. They tell themselves that, somehow, things will get better – *they have to.* But, you have to ask yourself: What are *you* doing to fix things? What more can you do to *help?*

If your company is struggling, what are *you* doing that is creative and courageous that will turn things around? If you aren't stepping up and volunteering ideas and strategies, you remain part of the problem, not the solution. To create more success for yourself (and others), decide to become part of the solution. You can make this decision if you are a senior manager, a junior manager or an entry-level employee. Just look at the situation from where you are and decide to make a contribution that will advance your company and, in the process, your career.

What Needs To Be Done?

I remember having lunch with a CEO who was complaining about people asking for promotions and pay raises. Her theory is this: If you do more work and create more responsibility for yourself, the promotion and pay raise will be automatic.

The more I talked to CEOs and other senior executives, the more I heard that theory. Almost all of them said they created more power and influence for themselves by identifying needs within their company that were not being addressed, then volunteering to handle the extra responsibility.

Companies love people who do that because they get more accomplished without having to make new hires. And, at a time like this? There is plenty of extra heavy lifting that needs to be done. What new assignments can you and your team handle? What interests you? Where can you shine?

Put your name on something. But make sure you are doing your assigned responsibilities first because, if you aren't, that is what will be noticed. If you can do your job and expand your influence by volunteering to help in another area, you will win clout and visibility. It is the ability to raise your hand and help when others are cowering in place that will set you apart from your peers. Granted, some managers are threatened by the overeager team member whose work will outshine everybody else, but this is a great moment to step forward and strut your stuff.

Spend a little time identifying the ten main difficulties that your company is confronting.

Always keep your eyes open for opportunities to stand up and lead – particularly in areas where nobody is eager to help. Your ingenuity and energy are needed now, and anything extra you do will make you more valuable to the company.

Finally, if you volunteer to do something, *deliver!* You are better off sitting there doing nothing than you are by identifying a problem, playing the hero and volunteering to fix it, then dropping the ball. If you are going to play in this arena, *own* this arena. Claim it with hard work, fresh ideas and the commitment to excellence that will definitely serve you well.

Leadership Touchpoints:

What exactly is the *job* you need to do? Knowing what the *real* work is will help you to lead without the distractions of personalities and politics.

Who are you serving, and what do they expect? Instead of focusing on what your boss wants or what your employees expect, ask yourself *who* you are serving. In most cases, it will be a *customer* or other *stakeholder.* Keep your true client's needs in mind as you develop your vision and steer the course.

Do you have the right people? There comes a point when you have to evaluate whether the team you have is the team that can score. Look at your people, figure out how to maximize their contributions and evaluate whether they are the right individuals to carry your vision forward so you can *deliver to the customer.* Remember, serving your customer or stockholder or other constituent is the only way you can deliver success to the people around you.

Are you communicating properly? Most people suffer some degree of paralysis in a climate where they are afraid of the unknown. How can you happily perform your best if you are worried that you might be laid off? Lay out your vision, show your people the milestones, and tell them the possibilities in a way that minimizes fear – but does not lie. If you can't say whether or not there will be layoffs, let them know *when* you might have more information to pass along.

Be a good person. Eventually, the bad guys always trip up. They get greedy or they take shortcuts or they screw people over and, even if it doesn't happen when we would like it to happen, the Karma Police will come and get them. It is a whole lot easier to succeed if you are succeeding as a human first, and as a business person second.

Every time you stray from your core values, you pay for it. If you compromise those values, you compromise your *self*. It's too expensive.

What Are You After?

There are legions of "leaders" out there desperately trying to keep their ships from sinking by plugging up this hole over here, then running over to the other side and plugging up that one before running up front to plug up the next one. Their ships are taking on so much water so fast that they don't think they have time to stand back and figure out the master plan. When the ship is going down, they don't have time to enjoy the luxury of analysis, goal-setting and benchmarks. They've got to plug up all those holes!

If that is how you've been handling your challenges, remember that you can't save a rapidly sinking ship by plugging up one leak at a time. You may not have time for all the test studies, arguments, focus groups, deliberation and reasoning that you used to experience when you were charting the course, but you must have time to always go back to the core questions that made you successful in the beginning, whether you are analyzing what to do for your company or for your career.

What are you after? Seriously, what are your goals? When you are pulled in many directions at one time, it is easy to forget the main challenges you face. At a time like this, it is vital that you know and that all of your people know what is expected. State the vision. Let your people know what they need to do, when they need to do it and how. Communicate! With the right goals, people, communication and inspiration, you can do *a lot* to keep your ship from going down.

It is too easy to get overwhelmed. I know what kind of stress people are dealing with, and the challenges are daunting. But, they don't have to be crushing. Step outside of the chaos for a minute and look at your situation as an opportunity to see what you are made of. This is your chance to do big things. Some of the things you try will work, and some won't. But you will emerge from these moments as a stronger leader, tested and proven.

Look at all the challenges you face. Get input from others to get perspective on which problems are most critical, then brainstorm solutions that can create the greatest results. At this point, you may well advance your career if you demonstrate brilliance and leadership in a moment of crisis, but you will do that best if you just do what needs to be done in the best way you can. You don't need to be selfish or ambitious in a time like this. Your leadership and performance automatically will propel your ambitions if you deliver. The magic right now comes with a bit of humility and altruism.

Over Communicate

The most shocking thing about other people is that a) They don't all think the way I do b) They aren't motivated by the same things that motivate me c) They don't perform the way I do and d) They aren't just like me.

I was astonished by human behavior in my first leadership experience when I ran a task force on media coverage of women and minorities. I had a dozen colleagues who wanted to help, and we met to figure out how to make things happen if we all did our bit. Everyone had an assignment that needed to be done in two weeks.

Two weeks came and only two people had done what they'd promised. I lamented this with the publisher of my newspaper.

"Do you have to repeat what people are supposed to be doing? Shouldn't you just have to say it once?"

"I consider myself lucky when I only have to say it three times," he said.

"Three times? You'd think the person would need another line of work if he or she needs to get the same instructions three times," I said.

He just laughed. If you tell someone what is expected three times and then they deliver it perfectly, what's the crime? Sometimes, people are confused about what is expected. Or they are distracted with other work. Sometimes, they make commitments and then forget the importance of the commitment – or forget the deadline.

A good leader communicates – and communicates and communicates and communicates. Especially now, when it is so important for others to deliver the best performance they possibly can. And, now, as people are so stressed out that they may not perceive messages the way they are intended. As a leader, it is your job to bring out the best in everyone. Even if they have quirks or come to work with different motivations and styles, *you* go to *them.* Not vice-versa.

Last night, I had dinner with a Wal-Mart executive who explained the whole rap on Generation X and Y workers who are more concerned with free time and self-satisfaction than playing by the old rules to which all of us Boomers conformed.

"I had one come to me and talk to me about flex time," she said. "I said, 'You want to come in at 8:30 and leave at 6:30?' And he said, 'I want to find a way to take off every other Friday.'"

In chimed a senior executive from a Fortune 10 company who told us that a young man responded by text message to accept a job offered to him by the company's CEO!

I started to "tsk" out loud about the bad form of these young people, but I was quickly shut down. The CEO welcomed that guy's text message, saying it's incumbent upon *us* to learn how to work with these younger generations, rather than forcing them to conform to our expectations.

The Wal-Mart exec changed my opinion even more. "I'll give it to these Gen X & Yers every time. The boomers are there at their desks working all day and all night every day and the young ones text this and do that with the computer and at 4:30 it is all done and it's perfect. So, WE have to find a way to work with THEM. They produce."

That's change. It's generational, it's cultural and it really takes an advanced soul to open up to it so easily because it is so absolutely radical to what we have always known. I never would have envisioned telling my boss I expected to get every other Friday off – *and getting it.* As a leader, my natural reaction would be to say to myself, "What a snot-nosed brat." But, we are operating in an ever-changing world where our ability to change and adapt will shape our ability to be effective and succeed.

I thought that executive was describing presumptuous work ethics of these young people. But her thinking had evolved far beyond mine. She saw their approach as different, and found a way to leave her realm to go into a younger realm to be effective. That is the mark of a good leader.

That kind of perspective is especially helpful at a time when you really need the best performance from all of your people. Of course it would be easier if everyone were as dependable as we think we are, but they are not. People are not always predicable or reliable – but a good leader plays to strengths rather than harps on weaknesses.

Have a vision, have a plan, then communicate it so the goals and expectations are perfectly clear. Check in. Ask questions. Make sure everyone is on task and the task will be done.

Inspire Them

I've had my share of good bosses over the years – and bad ones. Here's what I remember about the ones that were memorable as visionaries and leaders:

> 1. They were excited about what we were doing as a team.
>
> 2. They were excited about what *I* was doing as an individual. It is easy to get excited about my work when my boss is excited about it.
>
> 3. They valued mission more than ambition.
>
> 4. They didn't act like they were any better than the rest of us.
>
> 5. They knew that, when one of us dropped the ball, we felt bad enough and didn't need to be pounded on.
>
> 6. When we were overwhelmed with work and

they weren't busy, they rolled up their sleeves and pitched in.

7. They cared to ask how I was doing if I was going through a stressful time.

8. I felt like they knew me as a person, not just as an employee.

9. They didn't ream me out in front of other people.

10. It wasn't all about them – it was all about us.

I was lucky. I worked for people who recognized and nurtured my talents. I entered the workforce thinking I was going to be a simple feature writer who would write nice little stories about interesting people. There were no thoughts of being an investigative reporter, much less one whose work would change laws or send people to prison. I had no dreams of standing out. Good editors I worked with saw the possibility within me – and grew it. I would not be enjoying the life I have today if they had not expected much from me back when I didn't expect too much from myself.

They inspired me. They got me to love my work by showing me their love of their work. They showed me the potential of what we could do together – and the responsibility that came with it.

I often wonder how I might have been different if I hadn't had such great mentors who set high expectations for me, then helped me to meet them. You are in the position to mentor your colleagues in the same way that I was mentored. Whether you are in management or if you are sitting right across from a peer – you can bring out the best in others by being excited about the challenges ahead. If you are positive, others will buy into that positivism. If you are hopeful, others feel hope. If you pitch in, others don't resent having to do more.

This is a moment of shared sacrifice. It can bring out the worst in us if we focus on what we are losing and the doom and gloom that may lie ahead. Or, it can bring out the best in us if we consciously decide to give it our best.

You have so much power to bring out the best in others by giving the best of yourself.

Uplift Them

All you have to do is talk to a cross-section of your neighbors to see what the continued bad news has done to us as a nation. It has worn us out. We may be a tough and resilient people, but enough is enough. If you hear that your friends, relatives and neighbors are losing their jobs, their savings and their hopes and dreams, it wears on you. You can battle that by clinging to that spark of optimism that I am trying to keep alive here. And you have the insight that what you think is what you will create for yourself.

Again, if you think things are terrible, they will be terrible. If you think all is lost, all will be lost. If you think you are being brought down by all this negativity – just like the people around you – you will be brought down by the negativity.

But, you have the tools to avoid that. It can be done.

A good friend sent me an e-mail this morning telling me that he'd been laid off from his job and that he had no idea how he was going to pay his mortgage, much less pay for Christmas for his family. It was such a sad and heartfelt note and I sent my usual pick-me-up response. I have to be careful how I do it because there are times when a little too much optimism can rub folks the wrong way. But, I told him that he is in my prayers and asked him to focus on the one thing he can do for himself today that will move him forward. I reminded him that he is not in this alone and that he will get through it without being homeless and eating out of a garbage can. He wrote back that I'd made him smile.

All day, I have felt a little sadness pulling on me. I keep

thinking, "Oh no, not David too." I recounted all the friends who have lost their jobs in the last few weeks and I can't help but think the world is falling apart. And then...

SHUT UP!

Seriously!

SHUT UP!

I have to consciously bring myself back in line so that I can be productive and successful. If I focus on the darkness, I will find myself in darkness. If I remember that I am here to do good work and make a living, I will do good work and make a living.

We are no good to others if we get sucked into the negativity vortex. A huge part of leading through these moments is our ability to inspire hope and faith in other people. The world is desperate for the positive energy that will light the way back to good times. While those who are knocked down by adversity need a sympathetic ear from those in whom they confide, they don't need you to give them permission to wallow in their misery. Part of your gift will be your ability to give others the nudge they need to pick up and get on with things.

Be sensitive. You might be tempted to say, "Get your a** off the couch and start sending out resumes!" But the emotions of this collective experience are raw. What others need from you is more like this: "I know it is terrible. How can I help you out of this?" Or, "Let's go to that networking event Friday so you can start meeting people." Or, "You aren't going to be moving into the homeless shelter. You're smart. Now, let's figure out how we can use all those smarts in your head to put some money in your bank account."

Whether you are leading others from a position of authority and power or informally as a colleague, neighbor or friend, give them the best of you so they can find the best of themselves. The hope and support you inspire in them will change their lives.

View these important moments of connection as opportunities for you to give back to other people all the goodness that has come to you along the way.

Make Peace With Change

Six months ago, a former colleague of mine recommended someone we'd both worked with for a job with a major corporation based in the Tampa Bay area. His bosses loved her and offered her a great job for great money with great benefits.

She accepted.

A day later, she chickened out and rescinded her acceptance. She said she felt loyal to her job of 20 years.

Another day passed and she called back again. She'd thought about it some more and wondered if the offer was still good.

It wasn't.

Fast forward five months. She was called into her boss' office and laid off from her 20-year job. The severance package was pathetic. Now she is trying to figure out what to do with her life at a time when jobs are scarce and competition is fierce.

What had she been thinking when she turned that new job down? She'd already watched her company trim costs with a massive buyout and one round of layoffs. Her whole industry was slashing people like crazy. Why on earth did she stay with that losing situation?

She said it was loyalty, but I am sure it was fear. She thought she could count on her old company because her company could always count on her. She thought that, despite difficulties, old-timers would be protected from the layoffs. She thought her industry would rebound.

She was so lost in her own denial that she lost the opportunity to create a great new career at an opportune moment.

She feared change.

People cling to some delusional notion of "security" that does not exist today. They believe that familiarity plus longevity equals security, but that is so wrong. These days, there is plenty of evidence that there is no security out there.

I had a coaching session today with an unemployed man who is a natural for self-employment. He's got niche knowledge, great contacts, works like crazy and can do more in an hour than most people can do in a day. I urged him to finally put his talents to work for himself and start his own business.

"I'm really not the kind of person who chooses self-employment," he said.

"Why not? You'll make more money," I said.

"I like the security of a weekly paycheck," said the guy who'd just been laid off.

"Well, it doesn't look like your weekly paycheck was really all that secure," I answered.

If you are betting on a company taking care of you, think again. Maybe it will, but maybe it won't. No telling.

The only security you can bank on is *YOU.* Period.

If you know you are strong enough to handle any change and turn it into a win, then you have security. If you know that obstacles are inevitable and you will handle them with your brilliance and drive and commitment and shrewdness, you will have security. If you know that change is inevitable and you can master it – you will master it.

Be open and flexible, whether it comes to changing your routine, relationships or environments – or the way you do business.

Quick. Wake Up!

What happened to our quiet little world? Remember life before 9/11? We didn't know how easy we had it – even though we still thought we had problems. Then came a terrorist attack that made us realize we were vulnerable – even on our own soil. And then came the wars. Then the Wall Street debacles. Then, total economic collapse and more hardship than few of us have ever experienced. Things have unraveled so fast – and as soon as we accept and deal with one massive change, we get another. Nobody could have anticipated this much change happening at this rapid pace, but nonetheless, it happened.

Startled? Plenty of people are. In denial? You aren't alone. But, you have no choice but to get a grip. This is our new reality. This is the way our world is going to operate for a long, long time. The faster you get on board and define your place in this new paradigm, the faster you can rally and succeed. Watch the people around you and see where they are in a year or two. The people who developed the coping skills that let them pick up and move forward are the ones who ultimately will make money and find opportunity in this crisis. Those who keep waiting for things to change or get better will be left in the dust.

The speed and complexity of the changes we face these days can be daunting to even the most well-adjusted individuals. You've got to deal with cutbacks. New leaders. New technology. Offshore outsourcing. New laws. Fewer resources. Your job and your career are constantly in flux and that rate of change is exhausting. You can either whine about it or figure it out. Hopefully, some of these ideas will help you to figure it out.

Change Is Never-Ending

Twenty-five years ago, we were just starting to get answering machines and the ability to record television programs on tape. We were elated when FedEx would deliver a document across country in one day – and totally wowed when a fax machine could beat FedEx – and do it in a minute. Nobody had home computers or cell phones. Fifteen years ago, we barely knew what the Internet was. Somewhere in all of that change came the automated telephone systems that keep us holding forever before we get a human being. And conference calls. And offshore support from India and the Philippines.

Life *was* simpler way back when. It is not simple now. Believe me, I can't stand offshore support, I deplore automated telephone systems and I hate my cell phone, voice mail and e-mail. I totally despise conference calls. But, what good is it going to do me to hate these changes?

I can go back to relying on those little pink slips of paper the office clerks would hand me that said, "While you were out," but I'll be broke in a year.

Adapt and prosper.

Don't be stubborn. Right now, our nation is in crisis mode. What worked in the past is not working now, so the challenge is figuring out what we need to change, how to change it and how to do it NOW. Change must happen at every level, and as unsettling as all of this is, it *is* happening and you'd better make peace with it because life as you knew it is over and life as you know it is about to change completely.

When it comes to change:

• *Don't be too quick to dismiss other people and their wild ideas. There will be times when your own biases will stand in the way of your growth. Approach change with an open and receptive attitude so you can always be part of the solution – not the problem.*

• *People wrongly assume that status quo implies a certain degree of security. There is no security in this world – just look at the number of people who banked on it and were laid off. Security comes from within, knowing you can face any obstacle and adjust to any change.*

• *Even if you don't like what is going on, find a way to build your own success within the new constructs. What can you contribute? How can you make yourself more valuable?*

• *Always, always, always behave in a way that makes you viewed as key to future success, rather than as a relic.*

• *When news of change first comes down, stifle your initial reaction. You may be reacting to the fact that you don't like change in general, not to the actual change you are facing.*

• *Do not complain about what is going on to your colleagues. That will tag you as an impediment to your leader's success, and even if the change concept is misdirected, you don't want to be seen as a troublemaker.*

• *If you are asked for input, give it – constructively. Don't overdo it. Figure out what you can say that actually will make a difference, and voice your ideas in a way that creates an opportunity for you to take on more responsibility and help move things along.*

• *Your first job is to survive to fight another day. You might have the greatest ideas in the world, but it won't matter if you wind up labeled a naysayer, troublemaker or whiner. Choose the battles you can win, and fight them so you remain effective to fight again.*

• *If you disagree so completely with the change occurring around you, it may be time to pack up your talent and move on.*

As you find your footing in this challenging environment, make peace with this rapid-fire transformation. It's happening. It's going to continue to happen. Are you going to let change happen to you or are you going to get out in front of it, leading others and serving as a visible, viable contributor? It is a moment to make a huge mark. All of this insanity is unfolding like a movie. You can either be an extra standing in the background, a best supporting actor, or a star. The stars always know they have to stand out front.

Standing out means quickly accepting that the dynamics that used to work no longer apply, then studying the situation, coming up with a new plan, then adapting to the changes that will work for you.

If everyone is looking for business, who is going to get it? It's the person who has quickly adapted to the changing landscape and figured out where the business is. Be agile. Be flexible. Be open and be creative. This environment has created so many challenges and obstacles, but there are opportunities in those difficulties. Remember, if you aren't a part of the solution, you are part of the problem. Be a part of the solution!

About Change

1.Change *is*. Stop whining about it. There is no stopping the inevitable.

2.If you know what is coming, you can prepare, strategize and maximize the opportunity – rather than standing there all surprised.

3.Your star will rise if you figure it out, work it to your advantage and act as a contributor, not a naysayer.

So many people have lost their jobs to new technology or offshore support. How do you make yourself indispensable in a rapidly changing world like this? Do your homework.

Look at your computer. Your surroundings. Your work product. Your schedule. Chances are great that, ten years from now, just about everything you see right now will be completely different. If you find comfort in predictability, you are going to have a rough time riding this wave. The world is going to keep spinning at this pace -- with or without your permission. If you hear yourself whining, "If it ain't broke, don't fix it," you probably are one of those old cranks who just can't get with the program. You don't want to be in that category. Technology reshapes our world to continually devalue individual contribution. The only way to avoid it is to be ready for it and have another plan to make yourself indispensable.

> ## Look at your industry and ask yourself a few questions:
>
> *1. How has this company changed in the last decade? The last five years? The last year?*
>
> *2. Have you been in front of the change, riding along with the change, slowly and begrudgingly adapting to the change, or actively pushing against the change, arguing for things to go back to the way they were?*
>
> *3. How do you anticipate your company or industry changing in one, five and ten years?*
>
> *4. Have you actively studied and brainstormed the possibilities?*
>
> *5. Have you positioned yourself as a key player in the change strategy? How can you do that?*
>
> *6. Are you internally networked enough so you can make suggestions and volunteer for assignments?*
>
> *7. Are you active in your industry so you can benefit from hearing what other companies are doing?*
>
> *8. Are you a leader in your industry so you can help create the change scenarios that will define what's ahead?*

It doesn't matter whether you love or hate the massive change that comes with new technology. Time doesn't wait, change happens. And happens. And happens.

You can either take advantage of the opportunities that change brings, or stand there, helpless, letting others tell you what you have to do. Either look ahead and adapt, or keep waiting for things to go back to the way they were. Your choice. One way, you win. The other way, you get left behind. It is that simple.

It is always best to be prepared for change so you can master it, rather than find yourself standing there waiting for an announcement that will leave you surprised and guessing. You will do yourself a huge favor by pro-actively checking in with different sources that will help you to know what is coming in the days ahead. Be sure to monitor every resource that will give you the advantage of being fully prepared when change occurs.

Monitor:

Technology. It changes by the day, so don't let it surprise you. Make a deliberate effort to learn how technology will change your industry – long before it happens. You should always know what is going to happen that will change the way you do business. That way you can be the first to successfully master the technology.

Trends. Know your industry. If competing organizations are shaking things up and getting positive results, you can bet the trend is going to move in your direction. Watch your trade magazines and the websites for your industry's professional groups. Know what is happening and who is driving the change.

Committees and task forces. This is the place to know what senior leaders are considering – and give you a chance to have input. If you have a chance to volunteer for an assignment to a special committee, *take it!*

Gossip. Listen to what people are saying. Devise an informal system for rating the credibility of your sources. Just because somebody is wrong 80 percent of the time doesn't mean you ignore them. They may well have the most important piece of news right. And, just listen to gossip. Don't repeat it. It does not help your image to be known as a big blabbermouth.

Stockholder news. If your company's stock is publicly traded, buy at least one share! Then, go to the annual shareholder meeting and read the reports you get. It is amazing what you'll learn through presentations and you will also benefit greatly through the networking opportunities.

Going With The Flow

So many variables affect your work. Everything from office politics to the price of gas can force you to change the way you do business. You can stubbornly bury your feet in your old comfort zones, or you can make a mind shift. Change is so ever-present in this world. Grow up about it. Stop whining. You may have enjoyed your comfort zone back when things moved more slowly, but things don't move slowly any longer.

Change is more visible and rapid-fire as leaders jostle to protect their companies during tough times. They cut budgets, transfer resources, try new procedures, move people around, take things away, start using new jargon, announce new visions and continually shake things up in hopes of doing what they have to do in order to weather the storm. Sometimes, their decisions make sense immediately. Sometimes, they don't. Sometimes they sound absolutely stupid. Sometimes, things work out. Sometimes they don't.

If you aren't the rule-maker, your "buy-in" will be appreciated by those who are making all the change. It can be hard for them to get that buy-in, especially if the change is radical. You may be able to help influence change by giving useful feedback that might steer things another way, but there will be times when you have to conform in order to be viewed as a valuable team player.

The Earth used to revolve. Now it spins. It moves faster and faster. Those who "get" that, see trends and stand out front and take advantage of them. Those who don't just wait for things to go back the way they were, which they never will.

Stand Still, Get Left Behind

Change Affirmations
• *I embrace change.* • *Change challenges me to test my limits and grow my strengths.* • *I know I will succeed in the future because I have succeeded in the past.*

Thirty minutes before my shift ended on my last day on the job I'd had for eight years, a co-worker stopped by my desk to wish me well.

"You're lucky you're getting out of here," she said. "I've been here for 12 years and I have been miserable for the last ten."

Of course she was miserable there. Management treated her like she was a moron, giving her terrible assignments and hours. Clearly, they wanted her to go, but she had a union-protected job that gave her the immense job security that would allow her to stay and be miserable for decades.

"Don't be here when I come back to visit Denver next year," I told her. "You can leave, too."

My decision to leave my own union-protected, golden-handcuff, great-benefits job at that newspaper was so difficult that I almost didn't do it. What? Leave the "security" of a stable job with good benefits in a gorgeous city for the unknown at a new job without union protection or the kinds of benefits that protection would bring? A friend finally talked me into it, if just to enjoy the thrill of shaking things up a little. It turned out to be the greatest decision, the first step that put me on track for my career as an author and speaker.

Since then, I have become a real advocate for plunging into risk because it is the only way to see what you can do.

But, back then, I was hesitant about change because I didn't want to have to prove myself all over again. Every time I find myself in that position – and it happens even when you are self-employed – I have to remind myself that I am smart enough to succeed again.

"I've succeeded in the past. I'll succeed in the future."

Tell yourself that, and say it again and again.

Starting over really can be unnerving. It sure was after I left that secure job. One day, I was faxing something from the city desk in the new newsroom. The fax machine was the exact same model as the one in the newsroom I'd left on the other side of the country. I looked around and saw all those different faces and a completely different office environment, and it hit me that everything – every single thing – had changed in my life except for the fax machine.

I had to prove my credibility and competence all over again, something I didn't especially feel like doing. I had to work extra hours and be oh-so-sweet and take on committee assignments and other networking opportunities that kept me from what I really wanted to do -- my job.

But, it didn't take long before I adjusted to all the change and had my new rut to shake up. It was a good lesson, because the ability to make change gives you great power to shape your own reality.

Too many of us don't ever use that power.

Remember that old co-worker back in Colorado who told me how miserable she was? I hoped like heck that she'd finally find strength to pursue something else for her life. But, a dozen years have passed and I *still* see her byline in the newspaper, still on the stories nobody else would want.

She has a good paycheck, a month of vacation every year and great health insurance, but the tradeoff was that those goodies came with a steeper price than she imagined. She still has bosses who demean her and work that leaves her unfulfilled. She is on a career path that is literally leading nowhere, waiting this very minute for the official but much-expected announcement that the paper is ceasing publication.

She blew her prime on being so unhappy, doing unremarkable and unrewarding work and positioning herself for nothing else. Tough times will force her to change her world, and I wonder how she will face the prospect.

When you are stuck in a rut, it feels like the rut has power over you. Like, what you have is all you can possibly have. That is so not true! Recognize when you are stuck, then accept that things aren't going to change until you change them. Whether you make change within your current situation or you decide to move on, do something positive to shake things up. It's the same thing for a job that has turned sour as it is for a marriage that has turned sour. If you don't do anything to make it better, it won't get better on its own.

Roll With It

The best way to deal with the constant changes you are forced to accept is to see all of the madness as just another day on the roller coaster. Life is not going to be easy and you probably aren't going to ride the highs and lows with perfect results every time. That probably won't matter because things will change again in a day or two and you'll have another opportunity to adapt and redefine all over again.

Hang on, roll with it and just be happy if you don't fall off the coaster.

I wish things were as easy as they used to be. They aren't.

I wish things were stable. They aren't.

I wish we knew what to expect. We don't.

That is our new reality. What I do know is that my mother did not raise me to wimp out when things get tough. She had a life-threatening stroke when she was 66 that left her severely paralyzed. Every time she would rebound, she would fall or suffer some other setback that would force her back into rehab. I asked her how she could keep fighting when it kept getting harder and harder.

She said, "It's not about what knocks you down," she said. "It's about how you pick yourself up."

Change is now the norm. Circumstances keep changing and so do the rules. But, it doesn't matter what knocks you down.

What matters is how you pick yourself up.

Work the Room

I just got back from speaking at a corporate leadership event that was attended by the CEO, all of his direct reports and more than 300 mid-level managers and employees. There was a networking reception after the event, and all of the senior leaders stayed to mingle.

Since those senior leaders are people who make and break careers for others, I evaluated the networking going on to see if attendees were taking advantage of the remarkable access the event provided.

What I saw was one hell of a missed opportunity.

Almost every person in the room networked people they already knew. Some talked to new people who worked at their same level in other departments. And a few "risk-takers" dared to talk to people one level up. Virtually everybody avoided senior leadership because they were intimidated. They sensed it was safer and easier to talk to their equals than to people they thought were way higher on the food chain. What a mistake.

First, how often do they score a chance to go up and make an impression on the CEO? Almost never. How often can they mingle with the other senior people at the company? Almost never. There was so much power in that room and yet I only saw a handful of people make an active effort to connect with it. Two of the people approached the CEO together, as if they couldn't approach him without a chaperone. The rest of the time, the CEO and his go-to leaders were left to work the room themselves. The CEO did float around a little, but the other senior leaders talked amongst themselves.

Why wouldn't you take the chance to go meet the top brass and make a connection that can help you advance yourself?

If I were an employee in that position, I would have figured in advance who was coming and do a little background research. I'd be ready with something to say before I even got there. It would have been my personal goal to come out of that event with a networking lunch appointment with at least one person I didn't know who was at least two rungs higher than me.

It's Not What You Know

The painful truth is just like the cliché says: It's not what you know, but who.

I used to be offended by it. Now I just shrug. It's reality.

Back when my first book was being rejected everywhere, I decided to apply for some jobs. One was as a journalism instructor for Manatee Community College in my hometown of Bradenton, Florida.

I expected to easily land an interview for that job. I had real chops as a journalist. I had four Pulitzer Prize nominations and had written for *The Washington Post* and *U.S. News and World Report*. I'd been a staff writer for *The Miami Herald*. I had the requisite master's degree. And I'd taught college part-time for a dozen years, and even had taught graduate students. I had great reviews and great references. Finally, I'd graduated from that college, way back when.

Imagine the comedown I got when I didn't even get called for an interview.

Let me tell you, I was astounded. So stunned that I filed a public records request to check the qualifications of the person they did hire. The guy's "journalism experience" was hosting a once-a-week radio show in a small town in Iowa. But, he knew people in the department.

The fix was in.

It always is.

You can sit around and complain about favoritism being shown with people who have an inside track or you can get an inside track.

Maybe you don't like hearing that connections matter, but they do. It is the way things operate. People like doing business with people they know. It makes them comfortable. They know what to expect.

You're probably the same way. If you are looking for an auto mechanic, are you going to pick one that your friend recommends or a complete stranger? Do you pick your doctor by looking in the phone book or asking around? Do you refer business to people you can't vouch for or people you can?

So, get to know the right people.

There are always places to mingle with people who know people. Just start doing it.

Internal and External Networking

There are countless places where you can network inside your company and out. Try to take advantage of as many of these opportunities as possible.

Networking Within Your Company

Informal Networking: The office Christmas party. The softball team. A company blood drive. The company team at the breast cancer or AIDS or Alzheimer's Walk. All are incredible places to internally network in informal situations. These are the greatest networking moments because everyone is relaxed and connecting on a more personal level, so always get involved.

Formal Networking: Company announcements. Internal conferences. Training programs. Leadership events. Networking events. Be there. Be seen. Never pass up a chance for face time with senior leadership. If there is a retirement party, go. Work it. And what good is going if you don't talk to the key people? You want them to know you. You want them to know what you do. You want them to know you are going places.

Committee and task force assignments: What a great place to shine and gain access to people of influence who can help you along. But, know your place in these situations. Show your place on the team. Don't monopolize conversations. Position yourself as a visionary, not an unrestrained flake who monopolizes the floor. If they ask for a volunteer, be the best volunteer possible. Communicate regularly with them via memo – not e-mail -- so they remember how diligent and effective you are. Do the work, create the image, assume the role.

Networking Outside Your Company

The networking venues in the outside world are endless. You meet people when you get involved in charities or when you are out on your daily stroll. I constantly expand my network on airplanes and in hotels when I travel because there is a gold mine of connectivity out there in the real world. This morning, I met Coors' Vice President of Marketing Innovation while hailing a cab outside my hotel in Chicago. We shared a cab and now we're connected. Before I left, I met a woman coming back from a conference for workplace effectiveness and she knows the meeting planner doing next year's event. We swapped info. That is how the world works.

I tell people to make sure they are actively involved in their industry networking groups because those groups will have the first line on jobs in the industry and can help you find a better job when you are ready. They can mentor you because they know your business and what you are up against. They know the key people you may not know, and they will expand your network.

There are numerous general networking groups out there. You can join your local Chamber of Commerce or a group for new business owners or any number of networking groups, and you'll meet good people. Many of these groups are filled with people who are trying to get traction for their own businesses, and that's fine. I love those groups and recommend them – not as sources for great advancement (although you never know), but rather, as sources for commiseration. You'll meet great friends with whom you can share your challenges. Plus, many of these groups have fun people in them. Business and Professional Women is a great example of this. Most of the women in the group are trying to find their way in their businesses. But, they are so much fun to be around.

There is a great chance to network within civic groups because you do meet community leaders who have the connections you need. Rotary is a great example.

Finally, there are executive networking groups within many industries that give access and mentoring to people who need help on the way up. These groups may be expensive to join, but the contacts you meet can change your career trajectory dramatically. It is important to know people at other companies because you never know when you will want (or need) to make a change. Their friendship and opinions will guide you as you make decisions about what you should do for yourself. Their connections will help you find work when you need it.

If I were going to apply at that community college now, what would I do differently?

I would join the Rotary Club where the president is a member. I'd go to some events where the provost is speaking. I would talk to professors already in the department and offer myself up as a guest speaker – *before* I applied for anything. I might even teach a class so I could get to know everybody better.

The big thing here is to strategize in advance about whom you need to know, then come up with ways to wind up in the same place at the same time.

Mingling at Events

People are often shocked when I say that I find speaking to 2,000 people much easier than mingling at a neighborhood cocktail party where I don't know anybody. Fortunately, I have learned a few ways that we all can be effective in rooms filled with strangers.

First, you can gain a lot of ground when you realize a lot of other people are also uncomfortable in networking environments. Simply go up to the other person, shake his or her hand and find out where they are from, what they do or what they think of the political situation. Once you meet that person, slide into the role of introducer. That gives you a purpose and helps you to move through the room in a way that makes others curious about you. You introduce one person to the next.

Don't get trapped with one group of people. A huddle with a group is comfortable, but it limits your networking. Remember to keep moving through the room.

Again, when you get your face time with senior leaders, go it alone. It's a great self-branding experience.

Heading out for a mingle? Here's what to do:

1. Do your homework. Find the bios of the senior people who will be in attendance. Find some common ground on which you can connect. Maybe you are from the same town. Or you like the same sport. Maybe you graduated from the same college. If you need to bring a cheat sheet, do it and keep it with you so you can know what you are going to say when the moment arises.

2. Dress the part. Don't dress for the job you have; dress for the job you want.

3. Remember your business cards. It is amazing how many people either forget them or don't bring enough. You are networking. Bring cards! Duh.

4. Be bold. You have permission to go up and talk to anybody – ANYBODY! – especially at a networking reception. Don't tell the other person you are nervous meeting them. Don't gush all over them (although a little positive reinforcement is always good). Seem sure of yourself.

5. Shake on it. It seems like common sense, but there are a lot of people with limp-wristed wimp handshakes who need to find someone who knows what they are doing and spend ten minutes practicing. And, if you have one of those "Let me squeeze so hard I will break your bones" shakes, lighten up. People not only deplore your handshake, they talk about you afterward, mocking you for trying to outpower everybody with your shake.

6. You don't have to meet everybody. But, you do have to meet *somebody.* I know a shy businesswoman who knows she doesn't have the energy to meet a dozen people at a networking event, so she tells herself she just needs to meet three.

7. Always have your basic line memorized. I am so sick of hearing this being called the "elevator speech," but that's what it is. What can you say about in thirty seconds that tells people who you are, what you do and why they need to know you?

8. Have some conversation talking points. If you have a few things to discuss, that keeps you from sliding into one of those awkward conversation lulls where you are desperately searching for something to say. Just have a list of ten topics you can go to. And, personal is okay. Some of my best networking relationships have been built over discussions about dogs and cats. I am not kidding.

9. Remember, it's all about *them*, not you. If you want to make your connections interested in you, show them what is in it for them. What are you doing that is noteworthy to the other person? What do you know that will help them satisfy a professional need that they have? Who do you know in common? Find the connectors that make them realize you are a valuable contact.

10. Meet the wallflowers. That person standing alone in the corner? Go say hello. First, you never know who the person is or who they know. Second, it is good karma.

11. Don't monopolize others. Keep it moving. Especially at networking events, the goal is to work the room. You can't do it and the other person can't do it if you make one friend and only talk to each other. There is more time for conversations later.

12. Follow the "One Glass Rule." It doesn't matter how much everyone else is drinking. Really moderate yourself. People watch how much you drink. Keep it to a minimum.

13. Make a plan to reconnect. Ask the other person if you can send an e-mail or call to set up coffee or lunch. Then, follow up!

Denise Morrison, president of Campbell USA Soup, once explained to me how crucial networking was in propelling her own success. You can perform all you want, but you still need key relationships to make things happen. "Networking *is* working," she said. "It's part of your job."

When I first started doing it, I kept things professional. The more I've done it, the more I realized that networking is best when the bond is personal. Even when the relationship is business only, I try to make a human connection – a friendship – because that is much more gratifying to me. I've made some remarkable friends and have had some pretty wild adventures with people I have networked. They've helped my career, but that's just the bonus. More than anything, they've made my life much more fun.

Get out there and meet some people. You never know how they will change your world.

Exploit the Downturn

If you buy into what the media is telling you, this is a *terrible* time to start a business. Everything is failing. People aren't spending. It's awful out there!

The naysaying may appear to be true because millions of people are losing their jobs, homes and retirements. But, don't be blind to the possibility that this may also be an *extraordinary* time to start a business.

Like I keep saying, the window is wide open.

I was at dinner tonight with three incredible hair stylists. One of them, Bev, keeps me presentable when I am on the road. The other two – Evelyn and Debbie -- are her equally talented best friends. Evelyn used to be the boss of twenty salons and is a proven businesswoman. Her life partner, Debbie, taught Bev everything about creative hair design. These three women know hair and they know the business of hair.

And, all three hate their jobs.

Actually, Evelyn doesn't hate her job. She used to love her job, but then she got fired when the numbers of her twenty salons started to decline. Senior managers didn't blame the economy, they blamed *her*. After she left, the numbers got even worse, but that's not her problem. She currently doesn't have a job to love *or* hate. Not that the obstacle held her back for five minutes. She already has enrolled in business school and, weeks after the firing, has an offer to launch a four-salon franchise in our thriving county on the West Coast of Florida. It's a good offer, with a good future.

Still…

Something is eating at these women.

It's possibility.

They have each dreamed of taking their talents and creating a successful business, but none has ever had the courage to go ahead and do it. Debbie has hated her job for the eleven years she has worked there. Bev is over the daily dose of bull she gets from her current employer. And, again, Evelyn is about ready to sign on with the new franchise and use her expertise to make someone else rich.

They have spent years in the "What if?" zone. I tried to push them over into the "Why not?" arena. Why not pool their considerable and diverse talents and start their own salon together? Why not keep Debbie working for six months while Evelyn uses her business savvy to do the groundwork by finding the location, negotiating a killer deal, strategizing a marketing plan and executing everything with all the precision that drove her other salons to the top in the past? And, why not start this business with Bev, who has a huge client base?

Why not?

I couldn't figure out what was stopping them. They have the business know-how to create a thriving shop. They have the talent to make people come to them. They have the drive. They have the clients. They have wanted to do this forever. What is stopping them?

It is the same thing that has prevented so many of us from experiencing all the world will give us.

Fear. The unknown scares them.

Debbie admitted she had a huge fear of failing.

I asked her, "So what if you fail? What is the worst thing that can happen?"

We took a minute to ponder it. The worst thing that could happen is that they lose their investment and have to go back to doing what they are already doing. Debbie could easily go right back to the job she hates, making the same good money she is already making. Bev could easily take her clients to some other salon and make the same money she is already making. And Evelyn could find a job by simply snapping her fingers and saying she is ready to make somebody else rich again.

"I'm afraid of the risk," Debbie said.

I kept asking, "WHAT RISK?" The best-case scenario (and most likely because they are talented *and* brilliant *and* uniquely positioned by the current market conditions) is that they start a business and make it work. The worst-case scenario is they start a business, it fails, and then they go back to doing what they are doing. They'll lose some time and a little money, but they can always make more money. There is no risk!

(I should note here that my work has put me in contact with so many wealthy and successful people who seem to have the mantra, 'I can always make more money.' I *know* that confidence frees them to take chances. See? Law of Attraction.)

Seriously, what risk is there if the worst thing that happens is that you go back to your current status quo? You're out your financial investment, but there are ways to keep that in check. There is no life or death risk in this situation. Plus, there is the guaranteed benefit of having tried something new. It's called growth.

I asked them to turn off all negativity and, instead of looking for reasons to do nothing, search their brains for reasons why this is a *great* time to start a business.

If you can mute the negative, you will be shocked by the inverse positive that exists. The truth is, this desperate economy has created some very enticing conditions for smart business people. For the three women with the salon dream, it's all so obvious.

First, what do they bring to the equation? Talent, drive and commitment.

Second, what is happening in the market? People aren't getting their cut as frequently as they used to – but people are still getting their hair cut. People *must* get their hair cut. Hair GROWS! It will always grow. As long as it grows, people will need hair salons.

Why is this their moment to start a business? Because there are strip malls all over the country that are *desperate* for tenants. Many of those strip malls have empty salons with chairs and sinks and all of the necessary modifications just waiting for someone to open the doors and start snipping away.

Debbie saw all of those empty salons as proof that the timing was all wrong to go into business. If others failed, why would *she* do any better?

The answer is right there in those vacant buildings.

Hard times lead to easy bargains. The businesses that went under couldn't meet the price commitments they'd locked in when the economy was in better shape. Guess what? This bad economy has opened up some real opportunities to negotiate. Deals are everywhere.

Debbie said the usual rent investment for a salon would be at least $2,800 a month. I laughed. Because authors don't have built-in pension plans, my retirement has hinged on my real-estate investments. I am a suffering landlord and I know what the rental market is like. One house that rented for $1,200 just two years ago is bringing in $850 a month now – and I am lucky to be getting that. But, as a property owner, I want a decent tenant in my homes to make sure the places don't fall apart. *Any* income I get is better than the no income I would get from the place being empty.

Same goes for the commercial real-estate landlords with those old salons sitting vacant. Will Debbie have to pay the same $2,800 for rent that she would have had to pay two years ago? No! I am betting she and the others can lop off at least a grand from that number – if not more.

Where else can they save? Construction! If they want to do modifications, this is the time to do it. Contractors and repair people are desperate for work. Tiling, plumbing, electrical work – everything is cut-rate these days because there is not enough work out there. These entrepreneurs will pay a fraction of what they would have paid back when the market was hot.

We brainstormed a little more. They could even negotiate better deals on chairs and equipment. Of course they could! In a market like this, no one is buying. When you see stories on CNN saying that you can even negotiate prices at chain stores like Best Buy, you can pretty much figure that you can negotiate prices everywhere else. If every price is negotiable, negotiate!

"Advertising would be cheaper," Evelyn noted. Yes! Almost every media outlet is desperate for advertising.

Finally, the cost of labor is less. That is the saddest part of this equation. People are desperate for work and are working for far less than they are worth. Is it taking advantage of the situation when you are operating on a shoestring and can give someone a job and income when they currently have none? No.

Build your business with integrity and honor. Don't take advantage of people, but build your business wisely. If you can negotiate a cheap rent, negotiate a cheap rent. If you can save money on labor costs you have got to go for the savings. Remember, even if you aren't giving others what they would like, you *are* giving them what the market allows. Believe me, if I have a choice of getting paid no money or getting paid some money, I will always choose some money.

Remember that and look for ways to maximize the opportunities that the current economic climate creates for entrepreneurs.

Everyone was so excited at the table. I could see possibility in their eyes. And yet, there still was something making Debbie hesitate.

"I don't want to fail," she said again.

Nobody wants to fail. But, how will you ever test your limits if

---

Putting Your Business Risk in Context

How hard can you cut investment expenses to the minimum to ultimately give your business its greatest chance to take root? Where are the savings?

Think it through:

1. What are your five greatest expenses going to be?

2. Does this economic downturn give you greater leverage to negotiate reductions in those expenses?

3. If you create greater savings in the start-up costs of your business, will it translate to faster and greater profits once you open the doors?

4. If you wait until the economy turns around, will your investment costs make the possibility of launching a successful business prohibitive?

5. What's the worst thing that can happen? If this goes south, will you wind up homeless on the streets?

you don't fail a little? And, why even entertain the notion of "failure?" I have always said that if you give yourself an inch to fail – you will fail.

Debbie's father was an extremely successful businessman who built his career with the most minimal education – just primary school in England. He knew inside what it took to build a business and make it work. Debbie wondered if she could ever match his finesse. I asked her if she'd feel like a failure if she tried her hand at business and wasn't as successful as he'd been. She said she would.

Her father is 65 years old and brilliant. He did incredible things with his career.

"Does he love you?"

"Oh, absolutely," she said. "He'd do anything for me."

"Then, why not stop trying to match his success and start using him as the best resource you've got? Ask him to help you create a successful business plan. Bring him into it. He'd probably welcome the challenge and love the chance to help you."

You could see that the light was coming on.

I wonder what will come of that electric conversation at dinner tonight. I know that I got them thinking, but I only have the ability to make other people think. I can't make them act. I really hope they will take the next steps to build their business, partly because they promised me free haircuts for life, but mostly because it would be such an absolute shame to sacrifice all that possibility to fear. They really can succeed – if they allow themselves to succeed. They just need to open up.

Taking Advantage of Reality, Not People

It is more important to me to be a kind and decent person than it is to win in every negotiation. But, I do negotiate. I do make decisions based on price. I will always go with the lowest bidder who can deliver the quality I want.

This is the time to negotiate – hard – but don't be merciless. It is cruel and unconscionable to dangle a minuscule opportunity in front of someone who is too desperate to say no. But, negotiate. It is the reality of our times.

I was getting ready to paint the inside of one of my rental homes when my insurance agent begged me to consider her husband for any painting needs.

"He'll give you a *great* price," she said.

For me, house painting during the usual summer lull in my speaking business offered me a week of mindless work. There are times when that is very therapeutic to me. But, a little of that goes a long way – especially when it comes to painting trim around windows and doors. Her husband really needed the work, so I called him and asked him to stop by to give me a price for all of the trim work.

He told me he'd give me a great price to do the whole house. His estimate came in at $1,300, plus paint and equipment. It was a fair price – in the mid-range of what was being offered out there on Craigslist and in the local classified flyer. But, $1,300 was more than I wanted to spend for something I could do myself. So, I thanked him and told him I was going to do the painting myself.

He then dropped his $1,300 estimate down to $800.

The price was so low that I felt guilty hiring him at that price. I really didn't want to pay more than that because I had planned to do the work myself and hadn't planned to pay anything in the first place.

"It's a great price," he said.

"Yeah, but I don't want to take advantage of you. I can do it myself and …"

"You aren't taking advantage of me," he said. "If you do it

yourself, do you know how much money I will make this week? Nothing. If you take it at my price, at least I will bring home something."

He and his brother showed up the next morning and they finished it in a little over two days. They were elated, and so was I.

Everything we do in business these days must be considered in the context of today's reality. All of us are cutting back. We have to think before we spend and make choices that minimize what we are paying out. That means negotiating deals that aren't always the most lucrative for those with whom we are doing business. Keep it in context. As a businessperson, you are constantly making decisions that cost you money. Everything adds up. Your job is to make money in *spite* of the economy. That means working with what you've got.

It's like a vacant hotel room. Let's say a resort normally rents the room for $300 a night, but times are so tough, nobody is making reservations. If the option is to get $0 for the room or $125, they'll swallow deep and take the $125. Should you feel guilty for paying $125? No, because you wouldn't have been able to rent at that resort if it cost any more. So, even though you are taking advantage of a bad economy, you are actually helping the hotel because $125 is better than nothing.

Or, think of all the cars sitting on lots these days. You can go in and submit a ridiculously low offer and probably get the car of your dreams for substantially less than sticker cost. The dealership is not going to be thrilled because the profit is nowhere near what they wanted or expected. But, you got the car off the lot. That's the point. You may not be giving people what they want, but you have the right to make any offer and they have the right to refuse it.

Why pay top dollar in an economy where bargains can be negotiated? House hunters have their choice of some pretty fantastic homes that are listed at bargain prices today. If you have found a great house that sold two years ago for $400,000 and is currently on the market for $329,000, is there anything wrong with you for submitting an offer at $300,000? No! The sellers might go for it. That's how it works these days. Even though they will lose money on the deal, they have been waiting for more than a year for a deal – *any* deal. The longer they wait, the more they lose trying to find someone to take the albatross off their hands. Honor your budget and find the best house you can get for the money you have to spend.

And, again: The person on the other side of the table always has the right to reject any and all offers. They have a choice.

Always be respectful of the other person's dignity. You don't have to break their back. Try to make it win for you – *and* for them. Just put everything in context. What should the price be in today's economy? What's your budget?

As you negotiate for yourself, keep in mind that you have got to protect your own bottom line, and if you negotiate with others, you've got to expect that others will be low-balling and negotiating with you. Don't resent it. That's reality. You also have the right to say yes or no.

All of this negotiation may seem like people are exploiting a very bad situation, but the truth is, any opportunity that is created – even if the price is low – is opportunity that wouldn't otherwise exist. Even if you aren't paying what the other person would like, you are paying more than the big goose egg they would be collecting if you weren't paying at all. Are you taking advantage of a bad situation? No. You are adapting to today's reality. You might not even be in a position to get in the game if things weren't so tight.

Spend A Little

I do think that our economy's collapse has finally taught us some of the values our parents or grandparents got from the Great Depression and embraced throughout their lives. My parents and my aunts and uncles saved what they could and were never extravagant in their lifestyles – even though they all could have spent more.

Our generation grew up far more materialistic and grew to love and acquire lots of "things." Lots of people found debt a comfortable reality of life. I have plenty of friends who were only too happy to jump on offers of "No payments until next year!" or, "Buy now, pay later!" They'd buy furniture and huge television sets and take extravagant trips and figure all was well if they'd just keep up with their minimum payments.

Suddenly, people are afraid to spend *anything.* I was cycling past a number of outdoor cafes near my home recently and they were all empty. On Saturday. On a *sunny, Florida-perfect* Saturday. No customers. That said so much about the way things are and the way people are spending.

The less we spend, the worse the economy gets. I'm sure those cafes aren't staffed as fully as they once were. And so the restaurants aren't buying as much food and the suppliers and trucking companies are laying off people and… You know, it goes on and on. That's why we are in this big mess.

The Upside of the Downside

"When written in Chinese, the word 'crisis' is composed of two characters. One represents danger, and the other represents opportunity."

John F. Kennedy

"A pessimist sees the difficulty in every opportunity; an optimist sees the opportunity in every difficulty."

Winston Churchill

"I am not afraid of storms, for I am learning how to sail my ship."

Author Louisa May Alcott

"Sometimes we stare so long at a door that is closing that we see too late the one that is open."

Alexander Graham Bell

"Smooth seas do not make skillful sailors."

African Proverb

Frugality is a good thing for us as a culture, but if you are in a position to buy things right now, this is the time to do it. If you've lost your job or are in financial peril, this is not the time to be booking cruises or buying a bigger home. But, if you've got some money socked away and have plans that are working to keep the income flowing, this is a *great* time to spend a little. If you want a bigger house, *get it now.* When will property values be this low again? If you need a new car, *get it now.* Name your price. It hit me that "things" have never been so cheap when I was looking at the ads in the Sunday paper. You can buy the biggest LCD television for half of what it cost last year. There were at least a dozen *good* laptops for less than $500.

And, I keep getting e-mails about last-minute cruises. There were several leaving in the next six weeks where the cruise lines were offering 7-day trips for less than $250.

I feel for businesses that have to slash prices just to get things moving, but that is the way things are these days. I feel for homeowners who have to deal with lowball offers, but again, it's the new reality. There is no crime in taking advantage of the downturn because your spending money is exactly what the economy needs. And, don't worry. Prices will go back up. They always do.

Even if things are a little tight in your world, spend a little. If you don't take a vacation and don't do Christmas and don't ever treat yourself to dinner out, you will wind up with a bunker mentality that forces you to just "survive." That may serve you well as we wait for things to get better, but projections call for this to take awhile. Meanwhile, life hasn't stopped.

Years ago, I was contemplating a trip to Israel and told my Aunt that I was going to wait until things settled down. "If you wait until things settle down, you will never go to Israel," she said. So, I went. If I had waited, she would have been right. Things are worse now than they were back when I was worried about going there.

I have remembered that many times when it comes to making decisions to spend money when it might be better to sock it away. Back when I was a struggling author, I desperately wanted a sea kayak. The kayak and gear cost about $1,000, which I shouldn't have been throwing away. But, I thought about it. I said to myself, "When are you going to have time like this to go and use a kayak? It may be a recreational expense, but you need to do this now." And, I was right. I have never had the kind of time or freedom I had back then. I was young, strong and rarin' to go. That was exactly the time to buy a kayak.

So, look at your situation. Tighten up and don't spend more than you have to. But, if you have to make certain purchases, this is the time to buy. Don't be frivolous, but don't be afraid to live now.

Spend a little.

There is an upside to the downside.

Don't Let Security Be Your Dangerous Anchor

Several years ago, I weighed my options. Stay in Denver at a job I hated and continue working for an absolute jerk, or move back to Florida for a better job and more money – but work as an editor for a less prestigious newspaper. I was ready to bolt, then froze.

What was I doing? I had a union-protected job where I couldn't be fired. Five weeks of vacation, good money, great benefits and I got to live in Colorado, a state I loved that was filled with the best friends I'd ever had. I knew what I had where I was. I didn't know what I would be trading for in Florida. What if my new boss was an even bigger jerk? What if I was even *more* miserable?

I weighed the options with my friend Jill Gould, who said the words that changed my way of living forever.

"Don't let security be your dangerous anchor," she said.

"Don't let security be your dangerous anchor," she said again.

And then, one more time, with emphasis.

"Don't let security be your *dangerous* anchor," she said.

Then she said, "If you ain't doin' something, you're doin' nothing."

I can't imagine two more profound pieces of wisdom to guide us through turbulent times as we make the decisions that will determine where we go next.

I quit the job, moved to Florida, stayed in the new job for a year and a half and then found my way to this new, exciting, I-can't-believe-they-pay-me-to-do-this life as an author and speaker. None of this adventure would be mine if I'd clung to that union-protected job. Instead, I would have been stuck in an archaic job in a dying industry. A position that would have left me with no security whatsoever.

I see so many people clinging to what little security their jobs offer, not recognizing that the security is not real at all. Look at the behemoth companies collapsing in front of our eyes. There is no security in trusting institutions that have to put profits first and employees second. It's good to have faith in the companies you have loyally supported and buoyed with your talents, but don't have blind faith.

A friend called last night and lamented how much she deplores the work she is doing for a government agency that is so demanding of her time, energy and spirit that she knows she has neglected her husband and herself. And, for what? The security of a paycheck. She and I started our own businesses at the same time. I worked so hard to run fast enough to make mine take off. She seemed stuck to the floor and, finally, she called to tell me she'd given up and taken the safe and secure job that now makes her so miserable.

I told her that we make or break our success by walking a tightrope, much like they do in the circus.

"Those tightrope walkers don't look down because, if they do, they fall," I said.

Just see where you need to go, put one foot forward, then the next, and then keep moving. Don't look down.

"The problem for me was, I couldn't look up," she said.

It was the most concise explanation of the difference between success and failure. To succeed, you have to have faith in yourself so you can move forward with absolute certainty that you are on the right path.

Don't let security be your dangerous anchor.

For the most part, I think we fear our own power because acknowledging it requires us to take action. Taking action requires energy, stamina and confidence. Risk presents us with the possibility of failing. It's much easier to blend in with everybody else, all the fearful people who don't venture into their zones of discomfort.

I look back on the great cynics I have known in my life, and I have to admit they provided a great deal of entertainment for me with their smart-aleck remarks as we watched one of our peers dare to chase some cockamamie dream that none of us thought could possibly work. Years later, the cynics had done nothing new with their lives. But, look at what the visionaries did:

There was the night city editor who quit to open a restaurant. It wound up being an extremely successful steak chain that was franchised nationally. At the height of his success, he owned 25 of the restaurants himself.

There was the television assignment editor who left to go to medical school and now is a great doctor with a huge practice.

There was the reporter who left for law school and became quite well-known for civil rights work.

And when those dreams worked, those who stayed behind

doing nothing to advance themselves pondered the success of those who dared. They made snide remarks about the successful risk-takers, but it was so obvious they were jealous.

Risk in the Face of Uncertainty

Taking Stock

1. Looking back over the years, have you been more inclined to choose security over risk? Why?

2. Has that helped or hurt you in the long run?

3. Were your parents risk-takers or risk-averse? What messages did they give you about risk?

4. Have you missed out on opportunities because you were too settled or afraid to try something new?

5. Are you open to new things now?

6. What will it take for you to become more comfortable with uncertainty?

7. Do you have faith in yourself? How do you show it?

I've written three books based on interviews with famous leaders and trailblazers, exploring the lessons they learned the hard way. One topic came up repeatedly – and I wasn't the one bringing it up. When I would ask about how they found their own greatness, they all said it had to do with their ability to take risks and bet on themselves.

Risk.

The magic is always in the risk. You don't encounter huge opportunities for fame and fortune by slow dancing with the status quo. The greatest opportunities come from the risk. Maybe you take a transfer to a job or company and wind up in a job where you are completely unfamiliar with the territory.

Look at Meg Whitman, who went to eBay in 1998 when the company had 30 employees. She was technologically ignorant, but look what she did with it. She dove into her discomfort zone and soon was the most powerful woman in American business. When she stepped down as CEO, she was personally worth $1.4 *billion*. Imagine that. More than a billion in the bank.

You don't get what you don't go for and, if you wait until you are sure you know enough to master a particular risk so you have a 100 percent chance of success, the opportunity will be lost.

Say you were investing in Google. Would you have made more by buying in when it was just getting going and things were uncertain, or by investing in it now when Google owns the Internet? The greater the risk, the greater the chance for winning. Also, the greater the chance for losing.

BUT.

Every time you lose, you grow a little more. You learn every single time, so if you have done the learning you were supposed to do, the next decision should be better.

If you aren't failing a little, you aren't testing your limits.

If you are failing a lot, you aren't learning from what has gone wrong.

Put yourself out there. Realize that life is a continuous learning experience, so the wins and losses don't define you. The learning does. And, as you learn and grow, you will win even more.

If you hold back because you are afraid of losing what you've got, well, I have news for you. You might lose it anyway. Just look around you at all the people who bet on a sure thing, only to find it wasn't so sure after all.

Don't Wait for Perfect Timing

My first book was released the day before 9/11. I know something about having to force my success in a time of adversity. Days after the attack, I went for coffee with a woman I'd met through the National Association of Women Business Owners. She was about to open a day-care center for dogs -- a fairly new concept at the time. She'd paid the franchise fee, rented the space, hired the workers and spent her savings customizing her center with play areas and housing for the dogs.

Suddenly, the economic future looked dismal and she worried she was diving into a huge black hole.

"I don't know what to do," she said. "I'm supposed to open next week."

"There's nothing else you can do," I said. "Open next week."

So, she did. She opened and worked unbelievably hard and marketed herself. A year later, there was a waiting list for doggie day care. So many years have passed and her center is now *the* place for yuppie dogs in Tampa. My friend takes her English bulldog there – and pays $18 a day. For a dog!

While the day-care center owner worked her business, I worked mine. I would have much preferred to be marketing myself in good times when things would be easier, but I had no choice. Books literally have three months to take off before they come off the shelves, so I either had to sell it or let it die. I sold it.

If you wait for perfect timing to start your business, you will never start your business. If you wait until you know everything you could possibly need to know to handle a change in your life, you'll never make a change. There is always some negative that will rattle your nerves and make you question your judgment. Especially now, since things are so unpredictable.

How can you make peace with unpredictability? Accept it. And, accept the fact that there will be times when you make great decisions and times when you don't. Just move forward knowing you have the wherewithal to make anything work out in the long run. It is pretty unlikely that the risks you choose will kill you, so you've got a lot of room to operate.

So many of the business leaders I have interviewed tell stories of disastrous decisions or bad moves that they thought would kill their careers. The mistakes may have stalled them out, but they did not destroy them. If they recovered from a miscalculation or bad performance and ultimately prevailed, you can have faith that you can do it too.

So, if a "failure" won't kill you, what is stopping you?

False Security

Think of the millions of people who wrongly believed that twenty or thirty years with a company counted for something. They thought that the company would always be there for them because they were always there for the company. That was the assumption.

One of the harshest lessons of today's reality is that too many people banked on the wrong leaders and institutions, counting on them to return the loyalty that they'd always been shown. It is so disheartening. I see so many senior citizens who are frantic about their future because the value of their investment accounts has plummeted. And others who worry about pension funds that are underfunded. Then there is Social Security – oh, that's a good one. Any security there?

I had one friend give thirty-three years to a company that worked her hard and paid her fairly well. The time came for cuts and, surprise. They laid her off. After thirty-three years! She was only 57 years old, and out of work. Aside from the losses she sustained to her retirement plan, she was given thirty-three weeks of severance and one month of health insurance. But, the greatest indignity was that security went to her car and scraped off the parking sticker while she was being told she was laid off. She was then escorted out the building. Thirty-three years, and that's the treatment she got?

The cruelty of these times can be so discouraging. You can listen to one story after another that will cause you to lose faith and turn dark. Or you can realize the obvious lesson from all of this madness:

You can't count on an institution to take care of you. Not your company, your bank or even your government.

The good news is, you can count on yourself, and that gives you a lot to work with.

The idea of having someone else take responsibility for all of my security needs is really delicious. If someone else took responsibility for money and health and housing and everything else, I could go hang at the beach all day. Life would be good.

But, the only person I can count on 100 percent of the time is me. And, that is okay, because I know I am reliable. I know I am smart enough to get myself through a lot of difficulties. I know I will work hard. I know I will deliver.

I have a friend who's lived in a way that shows the pitfalls of an individual relinquishing total responsibility to someone else. She's a delightful woman who is funny as all get-out. She's been married to the same man forever and he dotes on her all day and all night.

This friend wanted me to go to California with her as she ran a marathon. I took care of the plane reservations; she was supposed to take care of the hotel and everything else. When we got on the plane, I asked what she'd figured out in terms of a rental car and she said, "We need a car?"

"You've got to be kidding me," I said. "What part of town are we staying in?"

"I don't know," she said, handing me the reservation confirmation.

"This is downtown," I said. "We need a car."

"Oh," she said. "I don't ever worry about these things because Gary handles them for me. I choose not to."

I made a phone call on our layover and booked a discount car for us. When we got on the second flight, I handed my friend the tour book for San Diego and told her, "Here is the guidebook and here is a map. Figure out where we are going to dinner."

She started whining. She told me she knew how to use a map but, "Gary does it for me."

"Well, you won't eat tonight if you don't read this map. Gary's not here and I'm not doing it."

She whined some more.

I pointed at the map and finally, she opened it up and located an interesting health food restaurant mentioned in the guidebook.

At dinner, I brought up the subject of how dependent she'd become on Gary, her husband of 25 years.

He does all maintenance around the house. He pays all the bills. He handles all the banking. He takes care of the insurance…

"What do you do?" I asked.

"The gardening," she said. She laughed. But, it was not funny.

That arrangement is fine if her husband lives forever, but he's not nearly as healthy as she is. He's already had one heart attack. He could go in an instant, and then what would she do?

"I don't know," she admitted. "But, I choose not to worry about it."

That is exactly what the American people have done with their careers. They have abdicated responsibility for security and survival to corporations and businesses that put the bottom line above the human element. Workers trusted their employers because they assumed their consistent and loyal service counted for something.

Instead of actively taking steps to protect themselves and their careers, they *chose* to ignore self-preservation and place their confidence in a corporate system that, by definition, puts business above people.

When tough times arrived, guess what? Loyal service didn't count for much.

And that is exactly how security became a very dangerous anchor.

How many people chose not to leave unfulfilling jobs just because they thought they had great pay and great benefits and job security? How many people have stayed in bad relationships, assuming they were secure, only to be dumped because their loved one wanted out? How many people have tended to everyone else's needs, wrongly assuming theirs would be tended to when the time came?

You can say life is not fair or you can take a look at what you have and feel a sense of power in knowing that, as rough as it gets, at least you can count on yourself.

You know whom you are dealing with. You know you won't betray yourself.

My motto is, "Fall down seven times, get up eight." When you fall down, who picks you up? It's YOU. That's a good thing. You know what to expect.

Granted, I know a lot of people who have lost faith in themselves and have suffered a real crisis in self-confidence because of the difficulties they are experiencing, and if you are one of them, pay attention: You can go into a negativity loop lamenting the unfairness of life or you can go to the one resource you have always had that can love you and nurture you and help you more than any other human being. That is you. Once you decide to pick up and count on yourself, you can do anything you believe you can do. That is not to say you won't experience your share of setbacks that test your mettle – you will. But if you believe you are strong enough, you can handle anything.

Yes, there is a lot of insecurity out there in the world today, but you can find the security within.

If You're Going Through Hell, Keep On Going

Looking back on it, it seems like a bad dream. I was on my bike, climbing more than 6,000 feet to the 10,800-foot summit of Colorado's Grand Mesa. I was in really lousy shape at the time – and it was the first day of Pedal the Peaks, what I'd chosen that year as my annual cycling vacation. The Grand Mesa was the most brutal mountain climb I'd ever experienced, and it was beating me.

My gang used to cling to the saying, "Death before SAG." The "SAG" was the "Support And Gear" vehicle that would pick up the riders who just weren't up to the challenge. I'd never sagged in my life, but this time it felt like the time had come. I felt terrible. I'd hated that ride, I hated those mountains. It did not feel like a vacation – not at all.

I knew I had to quit. But, how?

That brutal bike ride taught me so much. There is a way to quit and a way to persevere.

Once I accepted that I could not do the ride, I came up with a quitting strategy. It went like this: I had permission to quit, but I wouldn't stop until I had depleted every bit of energy I had. I would stop at the next aid station, and take a very long break. It wound up stretching to an hour and a half – more than I'd ever stopped on a day trip. My plan was to recover from my exhaustion, get back on my bike, go as far as I possibly could, *then* get in the SAG Wagon.

After that long break, I felt like I could go a few more miles. I decided to just keep moving until I could not move anymore. I told myself, "I have all day. There are eight hours until the sun goes down. I'll just do it one mile at a time." I'd ride a few miles, then stop. That worked for awhile, and then I had to stop every mile. As I did that, one SAG vehicle after another passed me, filled with those who had quit.

I crept toward the summit so slowly that, I swear, you probably could have walked around me. One mile at a time, I kept moving forward. The moment came when I looked down at my bike computer and saw that I was within two miles of the summit. Two miles. I knew I'd licked it. I wouldn't have to quit. Anybody can suffer through two more miles of misery.

I remember summiting the Grand Mesa in the early afternoon, getting off my bike, pouring an entire bottle of water over my head, then stretching out, flat on my back on the ground.

It had not been fun. I did not take in any of the breathtaking Rocky Mountain scenery and I did not enjoy that experience. I am not going to pretend that the life-changing lesson left me with feel-good memories all these years later. I still look back on that day and grimace, and I never went back to ride that route again.

Sometimes you encounter a mountain that really kicks you in the tail. It may be when you are out there on your road bike,

Feel Like Giving Up?

What to remind yourself when you are hitting the wall and feel like the universe is telling you to give up: *Adversity is only temporary. Things will get better, sooner or later. You are learning and growing, and the moment will come when everything makes sense. The obstacles you are experiencing will grow and define you as a stronger, more brilliant individual. See them for the opportunity they give you. Remain focused on your goal and just keep moving toward it.*

When you are ready to give up: *Delay the surrender! Decide to give it one more hour, one more day, one more round. Only quit when you realize you truly cannot persevere another minute, or when you realize you are on the wrong track and want to do something different.*

When it is okay to give up: *If you can say, "I don't want this anymore and I have no regrets," or, "This is not worth it to me," or, "It's time. I'm done," then give it one last push - just to make sure. Do another gut check. If you are still thinking you are done, you really may be done. But only quit when it is truly time to quit.*

but more than likely, it will be when life changes course for you, forcing you to question yourself, your abilities and your mettle. These days, life is handing down hard and sometimes cruel life lessons to millions of us. The experiences can shatter self-confidence and self-esteem. There is so much fear and self-doubt swirling in the air. This is an era of great personal devastation. If you have been kicked around in this economic mess, you have a choice of being a victim or a warrior.

I say you should heed Winston Churchill's advice: "If you're going through hell, keep on going."

When you want to self and quit. Once you quit on yourself, you might as well quit everything else.

Those moments of great self-doubt are profound test points that determine your own strength and fortitude. They determine whether you want to achieve your goals – or not. You have to assume that things never go as planned and obstacles will arise to make your challenge harder to achieve. Know that, so you can expect and accept the torture of temporary setbacks and failures. Then get back up on your bike and move on.

As you fight to continue on, remember: You never know how close you are to turning the corner until you actually turn it. All you can do is be determined and remain focused on moving forward. Take it one day at a time or even one minute at a time. Don't quit until you have to quit. When you finally do turn the corner, you will realize how much more your success means. That which comes hard is always more meaningful than that which comes easy.

Keep Moving Forward

Life is complicated, and what works for you might not work for me. When you find yourself at one of those life test points and feel your commitment to your goal starting to wane, you have to honor yourself. If you decide to persevere, do it because it is best for you. The same rule applies if you decide to quit. Don't give too much power away, worrying about what people will think if you quit, or ultimately "fail." These tests are all about what you learn in the process, not what you gain in the end.

People use their power in different ways. I don't judge those who quit, but I do applaud those who quit a challenge because it is the right option, not the easy option. Use the moment to build strength and character, not sacrifice it.

There are occasions when our greatest growth comes from making the hard decision to cut losses and move on. Let's say you launch a business and quickly start losing money. Time passes and you lose more money. It continues like that until you realize the hemorrhage won't stop until you either shut down or file bankruptcy. You prove nothing by sticking with an obvious loser. The boldest option is quitting before you are completely sucked under. But, get the information you need to know that your decision is made from the power of information and insight – not fear.

Or, in another case, let's say you have a real bully of a boss who is holding you back and making you miserable. He has made it clear he isn't going anywhere and you are stuck with him – probably for several years -- if you stay. You don't want to be pushed out, you know you didn't deserve the ordeal and it certainly isn't fair. You shouldn't have to leave. But, staying just gives him the power over your psychological well-being.

Ask yourself this: Which requires more confidence? Staying in a bad situation, or walking away? There are many situations where it is harder to quit.

Weak people encounter test points, stop what they are doing, let themselves feel bad, then slow down or quit altogether. Strong people see those moments for what they are: tests of stamina, creativity and willpower. They may ultimately choose to leave a losing situation, not because they are weak, but rather, because they are strong.

Smart People Survive

I've met so many people in the last year who have been laid off. Half seemed set on doing whatever it would take to find new employment and be successful again. The other half were too shell-shocked to do much of anything. All of these people were in their late forties to early sixties, and none could afford to be without employment for long. Many feared their age would make matters even worse for them as they competed for the few available openings in the workforce. What can I tell them to make them feel better?

At the risk of sounding insensitive…

Buck up!

Getting It Together

▪If you have suffered a blow, take a few days to sort through your emotions. Don't repress your anger. Have a pity party if you need one. Feel what you need to feel. Then, put those feelings in their place, because staying in a dark place will keep you from moving into the light.

▪Reach out to friends. Pride is an expensive commodity, so don't feel the need to sugar-coat what happened. Choose your confidants and tell the truth so you will have the support you need to come out of the situation.

▪Come up with a plan. Even if you have no idea, you can do certain things to keep yourself busy and moving forward. If you've lost your job, you can:

▪Do your resume.

▪Network with old bosses and colleagues. Commit to contacting a certain number of people every single day to keep yourself on course.

▪Schedule informational interviews with key people who can point you in a direction that will lead to opportunities for success.

▪Consider temporary employment or contract work.

▪Decide if you want to change direction. Sometimes, a good career jolt can be the impetus to do something you have always wanted to do but never had the time or courage to try. Do you have a business idea that you've been afraid to pursue? Is the universe telling you that this is your moment?

▪If you don't want to change course, identify your best prospects and design a marketing campaign specific to each one.

▪Do something every day that will move you closer to your goal.

▪Appear valuable and viable. Print up slick business cards with your name and contact information, and go to events where you can pass them out. Look your best. Be confident. That will make others have confidence in you.

I truly feel sympathy when I hear people lamenting their misfortune. A few of them are on the brink of losing their homes to this emergency, and I can't imagine the kind of stress they are experiencing. I have shared tears with them because it hurts me to see others hurt. And, I hate it when life proves that it can be unfair. These people worked so hard to be successful and thought they'd built secure careers, but they were sucker-punched by the economy.

The last thing they ever expected was to be forced to start all over – again – whether they wanted to or not.

If you are experiencing difficulties, there comes a point when you have got to get yourself together and stop wallowing in the crisis. If you don't get moving again – and quickly – your crisis will become a disaster. Then the disaster becomes a catastrophe.

How do you buck up when you feel so defeated? By remembering my motto, "Fall down seven times, get up eight." Think of that whenever you feel overwhelmed. You have to be stronger than your challenges. People often say that "God doesn't give you any more than you can handle," and I think there is truth to that.

One thing I am certain of is that perseverance is the measure of your resilience as a human. People always want to know *when* things will improve, *when* the economy will come back, *when* things will get easy again. The answer to that is very simple: Things will get better when they get better. The economy will come back when it comes back. And, things were never all that easy, so don't over-glamorize the past.

Not much of an answer? Well, it is the best that the universe will give you. You don't know if success is one mile or one hundred miles away, one day or one hundred days. You just have to have faith that you will get what you are after if you persevere and keep moving forward, regardless of how hard it seems.

You have to *know* you will rebound, stronger than ever. KNOW it. That requires the change in mindset that I have described here. Take ownership over your thoughts and you will take ownership over your future.

But, how do you do that when you have lost faith in yourself and in the institutions that once seemed so reliable? You chalk this hard moment up as another learning experience, because that is what life really is. A series of learning experiences where you are given the chance to define yourself as a human being.

If it looks like the elements are against you and that everything is going wrong, remember this: SMART PEOPLE SURVIVE. It is just a fact. You are smart enough to find new opportunities to succeed, so keep telling yourself that. Remind yourself that you have been successful in the past and you have the skills you need to be successful in the future. You may have lost a round, but you are not a loser. Don't act like one.

Your greatest success is ahead of you if you choose to manifest it. But, if you tell yourself how hard you have it, you will have it hard. If you tell yourself you aren't going to find work because of your age, you won't find work because of your age. If you think that money is running out, money is running out. But, if you think that you will be stronger than any hard times you experience, you are stronger than any hard times you experience.

When things get complicated, remember that you can handle whatever life throws at you. You can.

Sure, you may have moments of insecurity when you wonder if you are going to bottom out.

Whether that feeling is real or imagined, you can conquer it by knowing that you are talented and smart. You'll survive.

Smart people survive. Tell yourself that – all the time -- because then you will possess the faith that you will prevail *no matter what.* It is a fact. You may have to make some temporary adjustments in your behavior, finances, long-term goals or attitude, but you will get through any difficulties because you are smart enough to do it.

Smart people survive. That is why you can take risks. You know you will not wind up destitute. You know you have the stamina and internal resources to figure a way out of any setback.

Smart people survive. Think of all the superstar business leaders who once found themselves on the brink of ruin, only to keep fighting until they were richer and more successful than before.

You're smart. You will survive.

Stop Beating Yourself Up

One of my closest friends was fired from her job three years ago. Her boss was insane. She couldn't stand working for him. Her performance suffered and he fired her.

It amazes me that, so many years later, she still wears the black mark of that firing as a permanent scar. That sad moment in her professional history should have been put into storage years ago, but she thinks it is the first thing that defines who she is and what her career has been.

Sometimes, things don't work out. Oh well. Move forward.

I know another woman who senses she is about to get fired and is about to quickly hand in her notice so she won't have to say she was fired. I'm perplexed by that. With millions of people being laid off right now, there isn't any stigma to losing a job. The paper said 65,000 people lost their job yesterday.

I know several people who know they are going to have to give their homes back to the bank because they owe more than their homes are worth and they can't make their mortgage payments. They are horrified at the notion of foreclosure.

All of these people have told me they feel like failures.

They feel consumed by shame because they think imperfect performance means they are unworthy as individuals. But, we are all imperfect individuals here on earth to learn and grow as best we can. Don't define yourself by your difficulties; define yourself by your growth. If you are going through something that you feel is embarrassing, learn from it. You are getting an education in life.

Don't harp on the negative. Don't let a single setback define whether you are successful. Just learn, get it together and move on. Work. Work hard. Work until you exhaust yourself, but work until you work it out. In these difficult moments, it is hard to remember that what is happening to you happens to just about everybody at one time or another, or even several times.

When you invite doubt into your world, the doubt will cause you to lose confidence and focus. Especially when you feel you have taken a career slide, you have to refuse to let your doubts take hold.

If your career went straight up with no problems, you'd never fully appreciate your victories. When you pay for your victories with hard work, ingenuity and fortitude, they are hard-won and meaningful.

There will be moments when you may backslide to a place where you wonder if you ever will succeed again. We all have dark moments when the forces of nature all seem to be lined up against us, times when whatever we try doesn't work and it looks like we might really be about to bottom out.

Don't forget: You are your greatest asset, and whatever led you to succeed in the past will lead you to succeed in the future.

You are *not* a failure just because you may be struggling right now. If you have succeeded in the past, you are *still* a successful person – but you are being challenged and tested. Instead of thinking your time has passed and that you are on the downslide, think of the brainpower and energy you used in the past that created your initial success. Tap into that. Your success is what will create more success.

Start Doing SOMETHING

It is much too easy to fall into a depression when things go bad, and that slide is what makes it so hard to right the course quickly. It's hard to concentrate on success when you feel defeated. I can hammer again and again on the human truth that you manifest what you think, but me telling you to think positively when you feel so negative isn't much of a help. Instead, I will tell you now to think productively.

Get some space. Go to a place where you will not be interrupted, where you can think and strategize.

Set your course. Use your computer or a legal pad or a clean napkin to write down the first three objectives that you must achieve in order to move toward more successful and productive output. Under each of those objectives, list three steps you must take in order to achieve the milestones.

Define your first action steps. Then, build a grid or call up your calendar or to-do list, and plot out how you are going to spend the next two weeks achieving as much as you can from your list. Pack those two weeks as full as you possibly can and I assure you, you will be back on track once those weeks pass.

Take Care Of Yourself

The other thing you have to do is focus hard on your affirmations and self-care. Exercise every single day. I realize that, in tough times, exercise is frequently the last thing you want to do, but it is a proven fact that exercise affects mood and well-being. You want to feel better, go for a walk. Exercise also battles anxiety. Feeling stressed? Run up and down five or ten flights of steps. Get moving.

Dale Carnegie was the master of self-improvement training. His *How to Win Friends and Influence People* is the book I most commonly recommend to people struggling with workplace dynamics. The book came out in 1936, and is as on the mark today as it was back then. Another of his books, *How to Stop Worrying and Start Living,* is an excellent guide to putting worry in its place. Carnegie published a helpful outline of his anti-worry strategy. I love the outline because it saves so much time, but the funny part is what he wrote to summarize his chapter called "The Perfect Way to Conquer Worry." Under that chapter heading was just one word: Prayer.

I don't force religion on anybody, but I do believe that we should honor our spirituality, whether we find it individually through religion or meditation or anything that stops you long enough to connect with the powers outside of yourself. And, if ever there is a time to pray it is in those moments when you feel alone and a little desperate. So, connect.

Also, if you like saunas, get in the sauna. If you like hot tubs, get in the hot tub. If you like massages, get a massage. Do something to help your body relax and feel good.

Surround Yourself With Support

Your friends and family will get you there. That is a fact. Just don't expect others to notice you need their help and jump right in to rescue you. Sometimes, you need to ask for help. You need to be honest that you are going through a difficult phase. You need to let go of pride and admit that you need your friends and family to give extra to get you through something that is pounding on your morale and spirit.

Many of my male friends tell me they hate asking for help because it appears like a sign of weakness or failure. While I try not to embrace gender stereotypes, there are some that do stick. You know – like a guy refusing to ask for directions when he clearly is lost. And, if you are that lost man, I hope you will come to laugh at that trait and leave it behind, because pretending to be strong when you feel weak is a real weakness.

It does take courage to admit your vulnerabilities, but we all have our struggles and we do not need to be ashamed of them. Sometimes, our difficulties are our own fault, and sometimes they are not. But those who love us and believe in us do not care why something happened. They just want to be there for us to help us through the situation.

Don't get angry when someone fails to anticipate your needs. Some people are more nurturing than others. Some people are good mind-readers. Others are not. People who love and adore you will also disappoint you. You have to ask for help. Don't expect people to notice you are having a tough time, because they likely will be far more focused on their own challenges than yours. They also may assume that you don't want them to interfere. Don't take everything personally. Often times, no slight is intended. Let your loved ones know when you need extra love. Let your support group know when you need extra support.

Bring your loved ones closer in tough times. They will get you through the difficulties because they will believe in you – sometimes more than you believe in yourself.

Rewrite Your Negative Story

Instead of wallowing in self-doubt or self-pity, get on with things. Look at the stories you tell yourself about how you are struggling or failing, and see how ridiculous they are. Rewrite your story to include the triumph you will create out of your current challenges.

Your story is that you are a successful person who has to pick up and get on with things. Your story is that you know you are smart and savvy enough to fix this situation. Your story is that you are going to look back on this period in your life and realize that your temporary feelings of defeat will be replaced with victory because you have the courage to persevere when you feel broken. Plus, you'll be even smarter and more adept because you've gone

---

What to Say To Yourself As You Face Adversity

•*I have let go of all of my fear and I have never been more productive in my life.*

•*I know I am successful, and I am creating more success.*

•*The things that made me successful in the past will make me successful now.*

•*I am capable of anything as long as I remember how capable I am.*

•*I am smart, qualified and determined.*

•*I am going for it again.*

•*I will create even more success than I have experienced in the past.*

•*I am a warrior; I am not a victim.*

•*This difficult situation is temporary, and I am moving on with my permanent success.*

---

through this.

I learned so much the day I did that bike ride up that cruel mountain in Colorado. I learned that I was way tougher than I thought I was. I learned to stop, rest and recharge so I could continue on my course. And, I learned that any long, arduous battle can be won if taken one minute at a time.

Lick Your Wounds, Then Rally

In the last two weeks, eight of my relatives and close friends have checked in to let me know that they were laid off. All were successful career professionals between the ages of 45 and 60.

Before this insanity spell, the job losses I heard about were people in my audiences or distant acquaintances or statistics. Now this economy has stricken the people I know and love, and I know that the next round of job numbers that comes out of Washington will be far worse than anything predicted.

Still, I remain hopeful.

I want to share an e-mail that came last week because it shows the very human aspect of a single layoff.

"Well, the paper released another 17 employees from the news department yesterday, and, very sadly I share with you that this time I was not one of the lucky ones. The phone call came about noon yesterday and by 4 p.m. the career that I have loved so long and with all my heart and soul came abruptly to an end. The words can hardly cross out of my mouth today that I will no longer be the only thing in my life I have ever wanted to be: a photojournalist at this newspaper. I am still in shock and devastated. Three of the remaining photographers were let go yesterday – a trend that will likely continue 'til there are no more of us, or no more paper.

"My heart is broken, along with my spirit of the pride of having one of the best jobs in all the world – a job I truly treasured beyond my words. I keep hearing that life will go on. In time, maybe I will believe in that. Today I can only cry, and cry.

"Right now all I can say is that if you need anything that I can do to make some money to help me survive and pay my bills, I'm your girl. Housecleaning, yard work, errands run, dog sitting, babysitting --ANYTHING! -- please let me know. And if you or anyone you know is looking for the BEST PHOTOGRAPHER for any occasion -- please LET ME KNOW! Fortunately, over the summer I bought all new digital camera gear and, given my 25 years in the photo business -- I CAN DO ANYTHING!

"For all your love and support and prayers, I am as always so grateful. I need your strength now more than ever in my life to help me get through this."

I felt terrible for her. I had two other friends get laid off from the paper that day. There was nothing personal in those decisions. Just bottom-line cuts that satisfied the corporation and devastated its loyal workers.

The problem with my friend's e-mail is that she entered panic mode before turning on the shrewd side of her brain. First, this is not someone who is living paycheck to paycheck. She's got reserves and 40 weeks of severance. Second, if she starts out thinking she's going to need to baby-sit and clean houses, she's going to wind up needing to baby-sit and clean houses.

When the bottom falls out, think BIG. Think SMART.

DO NOT PANIC.

I told this friend to start thinking of the businesses that have laid off photographers and go right to them and scoop all the freelance work she can. This means public relations offices, governmental agencies, marketing offices and other businesses. The work did not go away – the jobs did.

A week after I got her e-mail, I was sitting on a plane next to a woman who owned a very successful public relations business. I asked her if I was right about an increase in freelance business. She said I absolutely was right and asked me to have my photographer friend contact her about doing freelance photography. And the copy editor friend who was laid off to contact her about freelance editing. And the writer friend to check in about some writing assignments.

If you find yourself suddenly having to restructure your career, catch your breath before you react. Get mad – really mad. And sad. Scream and yell if you want. Cry!

Lick your wounds, then pick yourself up and get back in the game. You will sink if you don't start swimming, so start swimming!

Go out and find the open window where opportunity exists for you. It does exist – somewhere. The one thing we know is that, when companies order mass layoffs, the jobs go away – but the work doesn't. Many will dump the extra work on those who are left behind, then hire freelancers to do the rest that must be done. If you find those opportunities, you can earn income doing what you know, plus get exposure to these companies so you will be considered for openings when things begin to improve.

Use your brain. You may feel defeated and down on yourself because of what is going on in your life, but don't forget that you still have your brain, you still have your talent, you still have your expertise and you still have you. You are your greatest asset, and this is the time to work it.

Waking Up In A Nightmare

We have all experienced a few shattering moments in our lives when we hoped that we would wake up and find out everything that happened had just been a bad dream – but it wasn't a dream. My heart is with you, because I know how bad it feels. I know that sense of helplessness and hopelessness. I am so sorry you have to deal with this.

I remember calling a friend after I'd decided to divorce my husband. I told her, "All of my hopes and dreams were built around our life together."

She responded, "Then you need to find new hopes and dreams."

She was not being flip. It was what I had to do in order to get on with my life.

You may have been laid off, demoted, transferred or treated poorly by your employer. It may be your significant other who is experiencing the difficulties. You may be facing horrible financial problems. Whatever the crisis, you have got to look it in the eye and get up and get moving. You can only blame life for victimizing you for so long. After awhile, you have to take the blame for victimizing yourself.

You only get a free pass for being miserable for a short time. Other people get tired of hearing your worries and woes if you aren't doing anything to help yourself.

So, you do get to take a moment to soak in what has happened in your life that has thrown you into chaos. Then, you have to pick yourself up and get focused and get busy.

Some of the mentors interviewed in my first two books handed me some coping skills that now serve me very well, and can help you. They taught me that we have a lot of control over how an obstacle affects us. We can either let a setback defeat us – or let it teach us. Some people minimize or maximize the drama. I say, go ahead and experience it. Feel it. Then, MOVE ON.

Look at your situation and consciously decide how much fretting is called for, then fret. When your allotted time is over, get on with your life.

These are tough times, and when we encounter difficulties, we will process them the way we process them. That means, what you do likely will be a little different from what I'd do and what I'd do likely would be a little different from what the next person would do. So, as you try to cope with change or adversity, remember to honor your needs and feel what you need to feel.

That said, there comes a point when you do have to buck up, get over it, let go, quit whining and get on with things. The brain is a pretty powerful tool and you can use it to help make a conscious decision to let go and move on. It really will help you along – if you let it.

When you encounter difficulties:

Don't go into denial when something bad happens. Acknowledge it. Size it up. Really look at it for what it is so you know whether you are reacting appropriately or not. On a scale of 1 to 10, with 10 being a serious health issue affecting you or a family member, where does this situation rate?

Remember your strength. Take a minute to remember some of the adversity you have encountered and conquered in the past. Make a list if you need to, but use your past victories as reminders that you have survived other difficulties and have the tools you need to get through this.

Feel terrible. Really terrible. Take a few hours or even a full day to crawl under the covers with a big box of Puffs and cry, whine, complain, condemn or do whatever else you need in order to fully acknowledge what has happened to you. Then, tell yourself this: "I've had my pity party. Now I'm coming up with a plan."

Devise a temporary action plan. This doesn't have to be the solution to your situation. It needs to be the solution to the hard feelings. The best way to get on track once something has derailed you is to find a track on which you can travel. What are the five things you can do to move yourself forward, make yourself feel better and help you get out of your funk?

Take care of your body. The worst thing you can do is neglect yourself as you go through a stressful period. Too often, you encounter hard times and stop exercising because you feel depressed. Well, what happens then? You feel even more depressed because you have stopped exercising and have deprived your body of the feel-good endorphins that normally propel you through your day. The better solution is to exercise twice as much!

Look at the calendar. Size up your situation and come up with a few benchmark deadlines for changing things and solving the problem. If you need to start looking for a job, give yourself three days (or whatever you'll really need) to do your resume and craft a great cover letter. Then set a deadline to get everything printed. Then, give yourself a week to identify potential target companies where you are going to market yourself. These deadlines and suggestions are just examples. The point is to use the calendar as a tool to lift you out of a bad place and take you to where you need to go.

Come up with a plan. Use some of the other suggestions you'll read here to come up with the plan that will create more success and opportunity for you out of this challenging moment.

Don't ignore the fact that you have hit a roadblock. Study it. Learn from it. Grow from it. These defining moments will shape your career and your soul. More than a career challenge, you are facing a life challenge – something that will give you better tools in your coping arsenal so you can stand up and face whatever comes your way next time. There is no need to shrug off the situation and pretend it didn't happen, but there is also no need to let it completely discombobulate you and hold you back from even greater success.

Starting Fresh

Do you ever notice how it is so hard to do the simple things that will lift you out of a funk? Like, you know that you feel better if you exercise, but you can't make yourself put on your shoes and go for a walk — not even to just go down the block. Or, you know that affirmations work and take no time at all, but you can't make yourself do them. So, you start off feeling' the blues and slide into a funk and wind up in a full-blown depression. Ten, twenty or fifty pounds later, you wonder what happened.

We have to consciously do everything we can to keep from sliding into the darkness. Too often we wait until it is too late. I had lunch with one of my best friends yesterday and she's on a real downswing into a depression. Let me note here: She is a therapist. So, when I started talking about what she needed to do to climb out of it, I was telling her things she already knew. She couldn't figure out why she couldn't take the tiny steps she'd need to take in order to begin feeling better.

Several years ago, I felt like I was sliding into a black hole when we realized my mother had Alzheimer's disease. She couldn't recognize my father as her husband – no matter what we said to convince her. A friend asked me to meet her at the beach at sunset with my kayak. We went three times in one week, and at the end of it, my perspective was back in check. Despite the darkness of the Alzheimer's, I came back into the light, and it wasn't that hard.

The people closest to me know the two magic words they need to say to me when I start feeling the blues: "Go kayaking." That usually snaps me right out of a funk because the Gulf of Mexico is so beautiful and, when times are tough, I always get a special visit from dolphins or manatees.

Have people around you who will give you that kick in the rear you need when you can't do it for yourself. Know what makes you happy, and have good friends to remind you to do what you need to do.

What is it that brings you joy? Is it nature? Children on a playground? The symphony? Art? Shopping? Old movies? Gardening? Sports? What is it that brings you into the moment, where you forget your troubles for a few minutes? Think about that and then immerse yourself in your joyous new mission. Go do some things you love to do.

My friend's husband was laid off right before Thanksgiving. He's out there trying so hard to get another job, killing himself to pound the pavement. She told him, "We've got money in the bank. You need to take a day and go golfing."

That is a wise woman. Some people shut down and do nothing to help themselves. Her husband is on the other extreme. He's running so fast and desperate that it is unhealthy.

"I'm afraid he's going to give himself a heart attack or a stroke," she said, and she is right. Stress will attack your health if you let it. So, find an escape that will help you to begin your recovery.

Life goes on. Breathe. Keep living. Balance.

I should note that my friend's husband found a job ten weeks later, which is a testament to his diligence and determination. Fantastic. But, he admits that he regrets that he didn't take time to play a few rounds of golf. He's got a cross-country move and a new job ahead of him, and now he's missed his chance.

Step Away From Your Desk

A couple of years ago, I had two major goals collapse in a single morning. First, I got a call that a book contract that seemed

Affirmations:
•*I'm going to take my power and recover as quickly as possible.*
•*I'm letting go and putting this behind me. Today is for me, and tomorrow I will get moving again.*
•*If this is the worst thing I have to worry about, it sure isn't much. (Then, start counting your blessings)*
•*I am a warrior, not a victim.*
•*I will turn this into my greatest success.*

a done deal was dead in the water. Then, I got a call from an expert who evaluated a consulting project that I'd spent weeks putting together with a colleague. The expert told me that my plan sucked. What made that day especially terrible was that I was paying triple mortgages because one of my real estate investments was vacant and the other wouldn't sell. I needed money – but everything had collapsed.

I wrote about the experience in my journal, knowing the day would come when I would use the material. Here's what I wrote:

"This is a terrible day. I don't feel like doing anything. I am discouraged and disgusted and blah, blah, blah, poor me. Why share this with you? Because there will be days when you feel as cruddy as I feel right now. I am going through the whole pity party of "why bother" and "screw this," and I am taking notes because there will come a day when my readers will relate to these emotions.

"I am also laughing at myself. Thank God I turned 40 a few years ago. That turning point gave me history and wisdom and the perspective I need in order to know that most of the difficulties I face are just temporary setbacks. Seriously, what are the odds that I will never get another contract? Or that I can't tweak that marketing plan and make it work? Zero. In my twenties, I would have given up altogether. In my thirties, I would have spent at least a week languishing in self-loathing over each setback.

"I am languishing right now, but it won't last for long. Yes, I'm ticked off and frustrated. But, I know I have to shift into recovery mode before I get on that easy downward spiral that presents itself whenever we feel defeated. The recovery process has two steps:

"First, I have to do a little work today. And, I only need to do the minimum – just enough to make me feel I was productive at something and was successful at it, even if it wasn't a banner career day. Second, I need to bag work early and get out of the office.

"Some days, you lose. That's just how it goes, because other days, you win. You can't enjoy the wins if you don't know the pain of losing, and if you have ever struggled to achieve something, you know it means so much more when you have battled defeat and still triumphed.

"Stop whining, I tell myself. Get over it. Whatever. I still feel incredibly grumpy right now. I'm going cycling. Bye."

Three hours later, I returned from my bike ride and started writing again.

"Okay, I am back. I feel terrific. Energized. I paid attention to what happened to me mentally while I was out there on my bicycle, so I could report back.

"I spent the first hour all angry and in knots, trying to figure out strategy, planning what to do next, kicking myself for feeling crappy, then saying more things that made me feel even more negative. I do have my negative moments, but not that many of them.

"I cycled hard and fast and let the workout begin to exhaust me. Once I started feeling the fatigue, I slowed down a little. I rode the scenic bike path right next to the Intracoastal Waterway, and I looked at the sun dancing on the water, like it does the last two hours before sunset. I watched the seabirds and saw some dolphins. I started to center myself with the beauty around me. Two of my friends called on my cell phone to see if I wanted to meet them for dinner, which I didn't, but I loved the fact that they asked me just when I needed a little good energy.

"It all reminded me that I am a very, very rich woman – and I am not talking about my bank account balances. Whatever good or bad happens in my career is really insignificant compared with the abundance that exists in my life, regardless of what happens in contract negotiations or marketing strategies.

"Sometimes you have to step away from your desk to know how truly successful you are."

Okay, now let me tell you how it all ended up.

I got a tenant for my rental house. I sold the house that wouldn't sell.

And, four months after that bad day, the dead-in-the-water book project was approved and I was hired to write "The NEW Woman Rules" for the Network of Executive Women. Not only did the group hire me to write the book, it also hired me to do a dozen speeches about it around the country. Every minute of that project was an absolute joy.

Sometimes, when it looks like all is lost, it isn't.

You can either wallow in your misery or go and live your life.

Know What You Know, Know What You Want

Don't leave it to other people to figure out what it is that you need to do with your career. Don't assume that if you simply present yourself as a capable and intelligent person, a boss, HR department or networking contact will look at you and decide which perfect opportunity is just right for you. Few will make the effort.

Why should they? YOU have to take charge of your life.

Seriously, why would anyone want to give a job to someone who doesn't know what he or she brings to the table? Why would it make sense to hire someone who doesn't even know what he or she wants to do?

These are the two fundamental questions that *must* be answered if you hope to make yourself marketable:

1.What do you know?

2. What do you want to do?

Answering those questions can be difficult, especially if you are looking for a life-change but not certain what your next calling might be. But, answering those questions is essential to your strategy for moving forward, whether you are forced to make changes by a layoff or whether you are making changes because it is just time to do something different.

It amazes me how many people are completely stumped when asked, "What are you looking for?" They know they are intelligent and skilled. They know what they *don't* want. But, they think someone they don't even know is going to look at them and do the hard life-planning that they need to do for themselves. They want an employer or a life coach or a recruiter to look at them and answer the questions that only they can answer.

If you can't figure it out, why do you think someone else can? Why do you think they would even bother?

Since it comes down to you, here are the ten steps to follow that will help you through the process:

Ten Steps to Career/Life Overhaul

How do you get the insight you need when you feel so clueless about what to do with your life? Just do it, one step at a time.

First: Figure out what you know. Sit down in a quiet place with a legal pad. Give yourself 30 minutes to write down *at least* 100 skills you have. That includes everything from people and management skills to creating spreadsheets with Excel. Don't stop to analyze what you are putting on your list. Just make a BIG list, and do it fast.

Second: Get input from others. Get five people who know you personally and professionally to give a list of your top skills as they see them and another list – with your top strengths.

Third: Review and revise. Spend time looking at the input from your friends and colleagues and see if you need to add or subtract things from your skills list.

Fourth: Split your list into thirds. Start on a new piece of paper. Or three. Your job is to take each item on your first list and sort into one of three categories: "Things I love," "Things that are okay for me," and "Things I would rather not spend my time doing." Spend about an hour doing this, becoming more familiar with your skills set and your skills preferences.

Fifth: Get professional advice. You can go to a professional recruiting company, a career coach or your local community college (my favorite option), where experts can look at your preferred skills set and match what you know and like to real jobs and career tracks. They will then show you how to take your experience and interests and incorporate them into a smokin' resume that will stand out.

Sixth: Start mingling. You may be circulating your resume through the usual career entry points like Monster.com, etc., but remember, this is still a world where who you know counts more than what you know. Now that you know what you are after, ask people who know your future industry to tell you who you need to get to know. You can write to those potential networking contacts and ask to stop by for a 20-minute informational interview. Put them at ease by saying you are *not* going to ask them for a job, but rather, for advice. If they see how incredible you are, they may know of a job that will work for you. And, they may make phone calls to people who can employ you. Relying on an online job search keeps you competing with thousands of people and puts you at risk for getting lost in a pile of resumes that is never carefully considered. Knowing the right people helps you to be considered individually, and that is well worth the effort.

Seventh: Make finding a job your new job. You want change? Go get it. Don't be content scouring the Internet for job postings because many of the best jobs are *never* posted. That has been the case historically, but it is especially the case now because any advertised opening will result in a flood of applications that a lot of employers don't want to deal with. Figure out which companies would have positions like what you are seeking and find out who the decision-makers are. Then, write great cover letters saying you want to introduce yourself. Do not send your resume with the first letter. Follow-up with a phone call saying that you just want to check in before sending a resume because you want to make sure it will be welcome. Then, send it. Call to see if they have everything they need and ask for more specifics on the outlook and timeframe. Wait a few weeks, and then call back.

Eighth: Stay on track. Every Monday, set out your goals for the week. Every morning, determine your goals for the day. Every evening, ask yourself, "What have I done today to move myself closer to achieving my goals?" Know what you are after and how you are going to get there. You don't have to be an expert on self-discipline and organization to be successful driving on your path. You just have to be focused. It is so simple. Every day, know what you need to do. Spend the day doing it. When the day ends, check in with yourself to see whether you've done it.

Ninth: Be certain, be positive. Be prepared to face obstacles and difficulties greater than you've ever experienced. If you find what you are looking for without being slapped around in the process, go buy a Powerball ticket because you are one of the truly lucky ones. But, many of us have found our greatest success after persevering through one apparent defeat after another. You never know what it is going to add up to or how it will work out. Since these *are* difficult times, it is especially important that you keep your mind from veering onto a downward negative spiral. So much of what you are going to create for yourself will be created in your own mind. If you expect trouble, you'll find it. If you expect success, you'll find it. Maybe not the way you expect to find it, but you will find it. Also, there will be many disappointments that have nothing to do with you. You might have the best qualifications in the world and get passed over for someone who is less qualified. There's no reason for it, so don't go negative. It's just the crazy world of employment.

Tenth: Enjoy the process. As excruciating as it might seem, you are in a life-defining moment. There will come a time when you look back on what happens now and recognize these hard struggles shaped you as a stronger human being. When you view everything from a big-picture perspective, your challenges are more meaningful and less stressful. You are finding out what you are made of – how great is that? You are being bold, not weak. You are going forward with strength, not fear. This is a good time

for you, whether it feels good or not. You are learning
who you are.

If you take time to figure out what you know and what you
want, you can manifest the kind of true success that will reward
you financially *and* emotionally. Separate yourself from the
legions of people who know they want a good career, but have
no idea what to ask for when it comes to specifics. They keep
waiting for other people to look at them and magically have all the
answers and opportunities. Employers are too busy to spend time
finding ways to satisfy your needs. They are looking for people
who can satisfy *their* needs. Your challenge is to know what you
can do, then present yourself to the right people who can put you
in the right place at the right time.

Don't let yourself get discouraged in this process. The world
is so open to you if you decide you deserve success. Go out and
make it happen.

Defining What You Know

I've stressed the importance of knowing what you know before
making a decision about what you want to do with your career.
Once you have a list of your skills, I suggest you beef it up by
visiting a complicated – yet amazing – website that is well worth
the trouble it takes to maneuver.

O*Net is a million bucks worth of information and help and
it's all free at www.onetcenter.org . Don't let the site intimidate
you. It baffles me every time I go there, but then I spend ten
minutes playing around with it and realize how remarkable this
career resource is. It will help you create the resume that will floor
potential employers. It will give you a greater understanding of
your vast expertise and abilities so you can drop that information
into conversations with people of influence. It shows you your
value outside the description of your current job.

Here's one way it does that: Go to the "O*net Online" area and

SALES REPRESENTATIVE:

TASKS

•Greet customers and ascertain what each customer wants or needs.

•Open and close cash registers, performing tasks such as counting money, separating charge slips, coupons, and vouchers, balancing cash drawers, and making deposits.

•Maintain knowledge of current sales and promotions, policies regarding payment and exchanges, and security practices.

•Compute sales prices, total purchases and receive and process cash or credit payment.

•Maintain records related to sales.

•Watch for and recognize security risks and thefts, and know how to prevent or handle these situations.

•Recommend, select, and help locate or obtain merchandise based on customer needs and desires.

•Answer questions regarding the store and its merchandise.

•Describe merchandise and explain use, operation, and care of merchandise to customers.

•Ticket, arrange and display merchandise to promote sales.

KNOWLEDGE

Customer and Personal Service — Knowledge of principles and processes for providing customer and personal services. This includes customer needs assessment, meeting quality standards for services, and evaluation of customer satisfaction.

Sales and Marketing — Knowledge of principles and methods for showing, promoting, and selling products or services. This includes marketing strategy and tactics, product demonstration, sales techniques, and sales control systems.

Administration and Management — Knowledge of business and management principles involved in strategic planning, resource allocation, human resources modeling, leadership technique, production methods, and coordination of people and resources.

Education and Training — Knowledge of principles and methods for curriculum and training design, teaching and instruction for individuals and groups, and the measurement of training effects.

Mathematics — Knowledge of arithmetic, algebra, geometry, calculus, statistics, and their applications.

English Language — Knowledge of the structure and content of the English language including the meaning and spelling of words, rules of composition, and grammar.

SKILLS

Active Listening — Giving full attention to what other people are saying, taking time to understand the points being made, asking questions as appropriate, and not interrupting at inappropriate times.

Mathematics — Using mathematics to solve problems.

Speaking — Talking to others to convey information effectively.

Social Perceptiveness — Being aware of others' reactions and understanding why they react as they do.

Critical Thinking — Using logic and reasoning to identify the strengths and weaknesses of alternative solutions, conclusions or approaches to problems.

Writing — Communicating effectively in writing as appropriate for the needs of the audience.

Judgment and Decision Making — Considering the relative costs and benefits of potential actions to choose the most appropriate one.

Instructing — Teaching others how to do something.

Reading Comprehension — Understanding written sentences and paragraphs in work related documents.

click on "find occupations." You can enter a keyword for your area of expertise and then watch this database spit out more perfectly worded descriptions than you could come up with in two weeks of intensive effort. It hands you everything. It makes you look like a genius. Use the information and it will make others want to hire you.

I want to show you an example of what it can give you because it shows the kind of information you will need to know as you market yourself. For example, I typed in "sales representative" as an occupation. O*net let me select from twenty related potential job matches, from which I selected "Sales Representatives, Services, All Others." What I got back would literally fill six pages of this book, but here is a greatly condensed version so you can see how this website eliminates resume brain drain by breaking down all of your skills, abilities, tasks and areas of expertise.

Again, what follows is condensed to *less than one-third* of what that website offered. But this shows the vast offerings that are instantly available. It gives a full list of skills that you might not think of to add to a resume:

There are plenty of books and websites telling you how to make a resume that stands out; use them. But, before you do your resume, do your homework so you know what you know, and have a grasp of what you have to advertise. This is a great way to start.

Put Yourself Out There

"If you want to read a very inspiring book, read Hard Won Wisdom." OPRAH WINFREY

"You're still using that quote?" a friend said to me, just a year after Oprah endorsed my book on her show.

Well, duh. I was using it a year later and I'm using it five years later and I will use it next year and probably every year until the day I retire. It is on all of my promotional materials and at the bottom of every e-mail I send. Why?

Because, I am not stupid.

I learned a long time ago that you advertise what you've got, because if you don't, no one is going to advertise it for you. If it is a plus, put it out there.

Before going on a date, I'll wash my hair, shave my legs, put on make-up, agonize over what to wear, *then* go out.

Why?

Because I'm not stupid.

Use what you've got.

If you are doing your resume, you don't list all your shortcomings, you list your strengths. Some people lie, and that can be a fatal error because liars trip up and get caught, and once they do, they are branded as liars forever. Lying is an expensive and unnecessary mistake.

But, that is not to say that you can't make maximize what you've got. Why do movie stars wear make-up? Because it makes them look their best. Why do car salespeople make sure the cars on their lots are washed? Because nobody wants to buy a dirty car. Why do professionals proofread their memos before distributing them? Because they don't want to look like idiots.

So, why are so many people so reluctant to spiff up their professional images to present themselves in their best light? Why do some people cringe at the thought of self-promotion? I used to be the worst self-promoter in history. If I would write a newspaper article that got positive letters from officials or the public, I would *never* share them with my bosses. If I got a major story because of my own ingenuity or sourcing, I would *never* point it out. I figured my good work would be recognized and rewarded. Sometimes it was, but often it wasn't.

It's rough out there. Competition is fierce. How are you going to make yourself stand out? By being able to articulate what you know and what you want. Be ready when you are asked, and show off the best you've got to offer.

Embrace Your Inner Wizard

Think of *The Wizard of Oz* and how Dorothy and Scarecrow and Tin Man and Cowardly Lion and Toto thought the wizard was the all-knowing, all-worthy and all-capable savior who could fix all of their problems.

Remember the moment they walked into his chamber and saw his huge image projected above them? They trembled, they shook, they feared – only to learn later that the massive head of the wizard calling down to them was only an illusion projected by an ordinary man who was hiding behind a curtain.

If they'd encountered that ordinary man in the first place, would they have seen him as such a force? No. Would everyone else have feared and revered him so? No. But the Wizard stands as a grand example of an individual presenting an imposing, powerful presence through calculated and extreme self-promotion.

Sometimes, we have to be wizardly as we go about our business.

I remember the story of Randy Gage, a popular speaker who tried to set up his speaking business years ago. He'd had enough money to get a catalog of his informational programs designed, but not enough to get it printed. He had no idea what he was going to do because he was flat broke. A potential customer called and asked Gage if he had a catalog he could send, and he didn't. All he had was the typeset copy.

But, Gage reacted brilliantly. "Sure. Do you have a fax?"

He faxed his typeset pages, the customer placed an order that gave Gage the money he needed to print the catalog and then he got his business rolling.

That is classic smoke and mirrors technique, and I *love* it.

If he were utterly truthful, he would have said, "Why, no. I have no catalog. I had only enough money to typeset the thing, and when I did that, it drained my bank account, and now that I am broke I am just getting ready to give up and close down. But, if you place an order with me, I can keep going!" And if he had said that, he would have been a moron.

Who on earth would have done business with him, knowing he was failing?

And who would have believed the Wizard over the rainbow in Oz if that short little man would have come out and proclaimed himself all-knowing and all-powerful?

You don't have to *volunteer* all of your problems and shortcomings. Why would you?

Before I started my speaking business, I was a starving author awaiting the publication of my first book. As I've said a million times, it was quite the obstacle course. I was running out of money. I knew that, to be a speaker, I would need fantastic promotional materials. But I had no money to be hiring designers for a logo, website, one-sheet, and business card. I had no money for expensive letterhead or custom folders. I had no money, period.

I knew I had to have the materials that would make me a "player" in the league with other speakers whom I would be up against when competing for a gig. What did I do? I studied design. I learned the software. I scoured the Internet to find the absolute cheapest printing companies that could do small runs for as little as possible. I figured out how to create a website. When it came to putting my website together, I knew one thing: People think that if you have a big website, you are a big deal. And, since I was a writer, I had a real advantage in that department. I really *could* crank out the content that would help me create a website of more than 20 pages. I made it so interesting and so full of helpful information that visitors to the site would send me e-mails telling me how much they enjoyed it.

Plus, it helped me look like I was the most brilliant speaker in the world. I didn't lie about anything, but I did portray myself in my best light.

I often tell the story of the impeccably dressed man in line in front of me in the rental car line. The guy looked like a CEO. His suit was gorgeous, his hands manicured, his hair so perfectly coiffed and professional. He seemed impatient as he waited for the keys to the Caddy he was renting, and I soon realized why. The clerk informed him that his debit card had been rejected, and that he'd need to have one with $250 still available on it. Furious, the man stormed out and got into *his* car – a beat-up jalopy that spewed smoke and exhaust as he screeched out of the parking lot.

I'm not sure whether the guy was dressed up for a job interview, going out to entertain a client or on some mission to swindle somebody. But, he knew how to create the illusion of power and position.

Don't sell yourself short. Maximize all of the positive aspects you have. Use them, milk them, advertise them. I absolutely do not advocate that you lie about yourself, because you win with authenticity and lose with lies. Don't sacrifice your integrity, but don't sell yourself short.

When you are doing your resume, you should run through the list of every possible task you completed and every qualification you exhibited on every job you have had. From that, write the best, most powerful description of your experience. But, don't lie. If you didn't do something, don't say you did.

When you need to create an impression of competence, present competence. Present professionalism. Present everything that puts you in your best light for the people you need to impress most. You can project a bigger image, and that image can still be truthful.

Just embrace your inner wizard.

You, The "Product"

These times can be real confidence killers – if you let them. That is a choice you have to make for yourself. To boost your self-confidence, remember all you know. Know all you've done. And, figure out what you are after.

When a contact asks "What's up?", the answer is *not* "nothing." It should be a pitch that sums up what you are doing and what you are after. It can be a story or just a few upbeat sentences that give the other person the opportunity to give you ideas, support or help.

At some point, you may feel that this necessary self-promotion makes you feel like you are marketing a product. Well, you are. You are your own brand. You want others to see you as capable and viable and employable. You want them to realize that, regardless of current circumstances, you are a real asset.

You are your own greatest asset, and you have to work it.

Don't let your own insecurities hold you back. I know there used to be a stigma attached to being laid off or fired, but there is no such stigma these days. You are in huge company. *Millions* of others are in your same situation, so hold your head high. And, I mean HIGH. Because you must find a way so you can stand taller than the others so you will be able to claim your next success. Be seen. Be visible. Be out there.

One of my college professors taught me that success is 50 percent know-how and 50 percent "show-how," meaning the image that we create about our competence and abilities is half of the game.

It is not enough to be smart and competent. You've got to show others why you stand out as so smart and competent that they need not look at anyone else for an opportunity.

Believe in yourself, put yourself out there and know what you know and what you want. Like the adage says, the hallway is long but the door will open.

Trust The Universe

I met a woman this morning whose husband has Stage Four lung cancer that has spread to his brain. I asked her if they have good insurance and she said, "We did. Then he lost his job."

An old friend's company filed for bankruptcy yesterday and today she wonders whether she will lose her house.

In the middle of a nightmare, you don't want to hear some Pollyanna telling you that "It's all happening for a reason" or "Someday, it'll all make sense."

But, it is all happening for a reason and someday, it all will make sense.

Unfortunately, you don't get that insight or wisdom when you are young because you haven't been around long enough to take a long view of life. But once you have lived awhile, you can look back at your obstacles and say, "Well, if this hadn't happened then that wouldn't have happened and then that wouldn't have happened and then that other thing wouldn't have happened, and if none of that wouldn't have happened, I wouldn't be here."

Sometimes, the purpose of the sequence of unfolding events is quickly apparent.

Two months ago, my friend Nancy was laid off from her job. Two days later, doctors told her that her mother needed Hospice care. She'd be there for her mother until the last moment – something she could never have done had she been working. She didn't know what she would do about money, but she was glad she didn't have to go to work.

More often, it takes time for the insanity of life's obstacles to appear sane. But, it will.

As you go through a challenging time, remember:

•Things have a way of working out.

•The quicker you accept what has happened, the sooner you can adapt and recover.

•Never let your mind operate out of lack. Always see your life as full of abundance – even when you experience difficulties.

•Keep moving forward with faith and certainty that better days are coming.

•Don't let negative thoughts invade your brain. Positive thoughts will lead you to positive results.

•When it gets bad, look around at all the people who have it so much worse.

My twists and turns have shown me that it can look like the bottom has fallen out – *really* fallen out – but ultimately, it hasn't. If I just hang in there, count my blessings and keep moving forward, every bit of adversity will add up to something big and great.

I remember how devastated I was by the bully boss who tried to derail my journalism career. He sat me down and towered over me as he said, "You will never be more than a reporter..." At the time, I couldn't understand why someone could be so cruel to me. Then again...

If he hadn't been a jerk, I wouldn't have left that job to go into management at the paper in Tampa. And if I hadn't gone into management and been so bad at it, I wouldn't have looked for a book to tell me how strong women could be effective leaders. And, if I hadn't looked for that book, I wouldn't have known there was a void in that market that I could fill by interviewing strong women leaders and writing what they'd learned. If I hadn't done those interviews, I wouldn't have been mentored to take risks, and I wouldn't have quit my job to write the book full-time. If my book hadn't been rejected by every major publisher, I likely would have gone back into journalism. But, since the book was rejected and it took me three years to get the thing published, I was open to a friend's suggestion that I consider being a professional speaker. If my book hadn't been published a day before 9/11, I would have been out competing for promotional time on television shows with hundreds of other authors out there trying to get attention for their books. But, since everyone else had given up and I was the only one out there, I got attention and even won a nod from Oprah. If I hadn't gotten the nod from Oprah, my speaking career would have sputtered along until I either made it or didn't. If I hadn't had the successful speaking career, I wouldn't have had the opportunity to sell so many books and make enough money so I wouldn't have to go back to work at a job in the newsroom.

It goes on and on, but it all starts with that bully boss who made me miserable for four years. And, here I am doing work that I absolutely love 100 percent of the time. None of this would have happened if those obstacles hadn't occurred.

Look at the obstacles in your past and see if they were ultimately like dominoes, all lined up so that when they fell, they would lead you to where you are right now. It feels inevitable that I would be an author and speaker, but it wasn't. It was never my plan. The dominoes lined up and, here I am. Every torturous setback that made me feel inadequate or foolish actually pushed me to my greatest happiness.

Back in my 30s, I didn't have as much of an adversity timeline to teach me that things do have a way of working out, so I lost a lot of energy to needless anxiety. When we're younger, obstacles come and are dealt with, one at a time. It's all about this or that problem, which must be handled today or tomorrow.

But, the older we get, the more it becomes obvious that, while we are experiencing difficulties, we also have a few good things happening. And, it is not until time passes and we look back and see how the good mixed with the bad that we understand that everything does seem to fall into place. One event leads to another and another that ultimately will lead to greater success and happiness – if we let it. But, it's not until we've gone through a series of problems that we see that everything adds up to something. Depending on how you approach life – positively or negatively – you will see that it all adds up to something good or bad. It really depends on how you look at it.

It's All About Perspective

Of course, part of this comes down to perspective and perseverance. If you have a negative attitude and quit before everything falls into place, you will see how those dominoes lined up to make you miserable. If I'd quit before my story played itself out, I could have blamed that bad boss for making me so miserable. I left a city I loved to move to Florida for a job that was such a bad match that I ultimately quit to write a book I couldn't get published. Oh well. It all worked out. It always does.

The whole domino theory makes no sense until you have persevered and made it to the other side of your adversity. Then you get to look back and see how marvelous all of those hardships were. How they led you to grow and succeed. When you are in the middle of the madness, it is easy to feel beaten up and discouraged.

It is almost programmed in people's heads to explain bad things away by simply saying, "Life is unfair."

What a pessimistic way to approach things.

I just say, "Life is." We learn and grow from everything we do. Things happen to us that we don't like, but they are the experiences that will ultimately shape us into who we are. We can blame the universe or learn from it.

When trouble comes, it is so easy to get discouraged. We usually don't get to choose our obstacles, but we do get to choose how we perceive and react to them. Life is only as dark as you make it. Bad things can happen, but you have to see the light in them.

I talked to one of my old mentors today. It is clear she is within days of being laid off and she has sent her resume out. We started talking about the ups and downs she's faced over the years. She told me about the time she got fired from a job when she was 40 years old. She had no money in reserve and she couldn't find work, so she took off to live in Guatemala for a year. She fell madly in love and had the time of her life.

"It was one of the best years I have ever had," she said. "And if I hadn't been fired, I wouldn't have had it. Now that I am looking at that, it makes me wonder if I am in for an adventure this time around."

Of course she is.

It's just a matter of perspective.

Have Faith In The Process

When my first book kept getting rejected, a friend told me, "Whatever happens is what's supposed to happen." Like my failing was ordained by the universe. Like it was all out of my control.

I have to admit, she really ticked me off. I wanted her to say what everybody else was saying. Things like, "It'll sell." "Hang in there." "It'll all work out."

She started talking about some New Age thing she was reading that made it seem like life plays out the way it is supposed to play out. Whatever happened was allegedly part of the universe's plan for me. She carried this out to such an extreme that she actually said we would find a parking space downtown if it was supposed to play out like that.

That sounded like the biggest crock to me!

The universe doesn't contemplate your need for a parking space.

Does it?

I have no idea.

But, do you ever notice how a string of coincidences will align like a constellation and position you for something incredible?

You hear the story of someone being delayed by miserable traffic and missing a flight that ultimately crashed.

There are times when the universe conspires to bring an incredible amount of good into our lives. We just have to learn to roll with it.

During the three years that I always refer to as my "starving author years," I noticed something. Every time I thought I was going to bottom out, something would happen to keep me going a little longer. I'd get an unexpected freelance assignment. One time, my insurance company sent me a $500 refund! Another time, the county bought an easement off the back of my property. Right after my first book came out, I was truly out of cash. A community leader threw a book party for me and told me to bring books to sell. I sold $1,200 worth of books – and that was a mortgage payment. There was always something that kept me from going under.

Have faith. The ks out in the end. Know that, and take it one day at a time.

Don't Look Desperate

When I interviewed Academy Award-winner Frances McDormand a few years ago, she talked about the lean years in her career and the lesson she learned that helped her to win auditions. If she looked desperate at an audition, she never got the part. People don't like to help desperate people.

She learned to go to auditions with confidence, presenting herself as a professional who would like to get the part, but one who would not die if she didn't get it.

I've always remembered that.

I am not sure why it is true, but it is. Desperation makes others uncomfortable. Even though most people like to help, real desperation is off-putting. Those who exhibit it come off as too needy, too clingy, too *something.* So, keep your desperation in check. Cool it. You don't have to display all of your anxieties and difficulties for the whole world.

A woman came up to me after an event recently and asked me how often she should follow up after sending her resume to a company. I suggested calling right after sending it out, then following up every two weeks.

"Really?" she said. "Maybe that is why the woman never calls me back. I've been leaving messages every two days."

Think about it. Would the person who calls every two days wind up at the top of your list? No. You'd see her as annoying. You'd think she had no other options. You'd think she was desperate because no one else wanted to hire her.

Cope. Adapt. Recover.

Whatever is going on, your ability to cope, adapt and then recover will carry you out of your difficulties faster than if you simply languish in the darkness.

There is a chapter in this book that tells you to go ahead and lick your wounds.

But, while you are doing that, try to have faith. Remember that things are not always as dark as they appear. In the long run, life starts to make sense.

Cope, adapt and recover so you can move on to the next thing, and then the next, and finally gain the perspective that shows you it all makes sense.

It is a very hard thing to let go of a familiar and comfortable reality, whether the crisis you face is the illness of a loved one or the loss of a job. You can spend weeks, months or years lamenting what you have lost, or you can get on with the business of living. Doing that entails a mature and mindful acceptance that things will never be like they used to be. Life will continue to test you – and it will make the tests harder.

You can handle it.

As you face these challenges, remember that things rarely makes sense while you are in the middle of adversity. Wait. Let things unfold. The universe does take care of you – if you let it.

Conclusion

You made it through last year. You'll make it through this one.

How?

Cope and adapt, and you will profit greatly. Freeze up in fear or anger and you become just another victim of circumstances, creating opportunities for those of us who refuse to surrender.

When everyone else gives up, the window is wide open for those of us who persevere. Persevere.

When you feel yourself going negative, turn off your brain. Take charge of it. Don't waste a single day of your life, because time is always precious. No one is on earth forever, and whether you are experiencing ease or adversity, you can enjoy what you have.

Count your blessings, then count them again. That will keep you grounded.

There is so much possibility out there for you – if only you believe it exists. You just have to make up your mind to replace negativity with hope, inaction with innovation.

No, these are not the best financial circumstances.

But work 'em, just the same.

When you feel worn out, remember to slow down and breathe deeply, grateful that you are safe and secure in who you are, sure that you can handle anything if you just take life a day at a time. You will get past any adversity. You are smart. Smart people survive.

No matter what.

It's all about perspective. When I go to bed at night, I imagine earth, from above. There are 6.7 billion people down here and every single one of us thinks that the world begins and ends right where we stand. We think our problems are huge, but usually, they aren't. Not when you look at what others face.

Why worry what tomorrow might bring when you are living right now, in this moment? Things will work out. They will.

We are simply here on this earth to live our lives. Maybe we are going through these tough times so that we remember it is love and nature and life that matter most. Those are the things that endure.

When it seems like everything is going all wrong, it's hard to see that you're really all right.

But, you are.

Fawn's Speaking

Why are America's largest corporations hiring Fawn Germer to speak at a time when they are slashing budgets? Because Fawn knows how to change performance dynamics to deliver the best results in the toughest times.

Fawn is one of the nation's most sought-after leadership keynote speakers. This four-time Pulitzer-nominated journalist has personally interviewed more of the world's greatest leaders than any other speaker in America. From those leaders, she learned how to take advantage of adversity and use it as a defining moment for leadership. She is the best-selling author of five books, and a former writer for *The Washington Post*, *U.S. News and World Report* and *The Miami Herald*.

Fawn regularly meets with the nation's corporate leaders to find out what they are doing to turn things around. Their insights shape what she teaches her audiences, showing individuals how to focus on results-driven solutions and opportunities rather than surrendering to a victim mindset.

Nationally, we have a fearful, beleaguered workforce. While senior executives figure out ways to cut here and add there, they will turn to those who hyper-perform, over-deliver and come up with new ideas for a changing landscape. Instead of cowering, it is the moment where we must muster courage and ingenuity to rise above. Fawn inspires her audiences to do that by identifying exactly what they can contribute and diving right in to help.

Her clients include Kraft, Coca-Cola, Ford Motor Co., Accenture, Genworth Financial, SAP, Exelon, 3m, Motorola, Intel, PepsiCo, KPMG, Boeing, GlaxoSmithKline, Novartis, Cytec, Lifetime Television – and many others.

Why Great Leaders Listen to Fawn

"Fawn Germer has the uncanny ability to capture an audience at every touchpoint possible. She is smart, witty, charming, challenging, thought provoking, and engaging – all at the same time. She captures both the mind and the heart by inspiring men and women not just to go for the gold, but to get it! I know. I went for it and I got it!"
Barb Hartman, *fmr. Vice President, Customer Business Development, Procter and Gamble*

"Fawn has the gift of finding the truth below the facts and telling it in ways that enable people to act. Because she is fearless and relentless she gets both the big picture and local action. She lives with the motto, "Never let a crisis be wasted - in the crisis is an opportunity to grab"."
Steffie Allen, *Principle, The Athena Group, LLC*

"Fawn Germer made our night of Hard Won Wisdom one of the most successful events ever held at the Swiss Embassy. It was a memorable night filled with fresh thought and vision, and it worked because her comfort with the audience made us so comfortable with her."
Carlos Orga, *Embassy of Switzerland, Minister, Presence Switzerland*

"Fawn takes the time to understand the audience and appropriately craft her message. She has a huge knowledge base to draw from and is willing to get creative when working with the group so that her delivery is spot on. Fawn is always engaging, thoughtful and inspiring."
Liz Corey, *Director of Organizational Development and Training, Global Imaging Systems, fmr. Senior Talent Manager, Harris Corporation*

"Fawn weaves a gripping personal tale into the leadership lesson and has everyone on the edge of their seat. She is warm, engaging, and builds lasting friendships from her associations. I highly recommend Fawn and would hire her again in a heartbeat."
Robin Rodin,*Principle, The Rodin Group, fmr. Director of eadership Development for GlaxoSmithKline*

"Fawn is a speaker who stirs your soul. As you listen to her story and to the insights of the amazing people she has interviewed, you can easily internalize the message into your own life. She is easy to relate to, because she is so real."
Kara Pelecky, *Senior Manager of Infrastructure Projects, Exelon*

"Fawn taught me that it is ok to take risks, even when everybody else thinks you are nuts. Break the rules, beat the odds, live your dream --that's Fawn's mantra and it's infectious. She motivates through truth and wisdom--- and what makes her better than the rest is that she infuses humor in her stories and is willing to show that she, too, has a vulnerable side."
Renee Warmack, D*ocumentary Filmmaker.*

"In these turbulent times, Fawn's insight is priceless. Read Finding the UP in the Downturn and unlock the secrets of moving ahead in today's volatile business environment."
Joan Toth, *Executive Director, Network of Executive Women*

"Fawn Germer is an inspiration! Fawn connects, inspires and motivates people to do the best that they can do in their own industry, field and community. If you want to read some of her jewels of wisdom - pick up one of Fawn's books. If the opportunity is presented to listen to Fawn speak - TAKE IT!"
Keri Douglas, *fmr. Press Secretary, Embassy of Switzerland*

"Fawn is one of the smartest and most positive people I have ever met. Over the ten years I have known her she has been an amazing resource, offering perceptive insights, strategies and encouragement, all wrapped up in her unfailing good humor and dynamic style."
Nancy Rawlinson, *Editor, Madison magazine*

"Fawn is a wonderful author, speaker and friend who the Network of Executive Women considers one of its greatest supporters. We hired Fawn to write a book about the amazing women leaders of our industry—a real turning point for our organization— as we published it and sold over 15,000 copies! Fawn has been a key partner touring the country and facilitating panels of the women featured in the book at our various regional events… Fawn continues to be a source of inspiration, ideas and support for the Network—she embodies our ideals of diversity, inclusion, and finding one's voice."
Alison Kenney Paul, *President, Network of Executive Women*

"Fawn defines the word inspirational. I have heard her speak to audiences of +350 men and women and have them laugh, cry, get fired up, and leave determined to take a risk and dare to push their limits. She can pull this off because her own story is so inspirational and she really tells it from her heart.*"*
Maria Edelson, *Vice President of Sales, Sales, Evenflo Company, fmr. Director, Customer Business Development Procter & Gamble*